Making and Using
INEXPENSIVE CLASSROOM MEDIA

by Betty Jane Wagner and E. Arthur Stunard
with the editors of LEARNING magazine

LEARNING Handbooks
530 University Avenue
Palo Alto, California 94301

Foreword

Inexpensive materials and audio-visual equipment found in most schools can prove invaluable to teachers and students for preserving, displaying and presenting ideas and projects. The step-by-step directions in this handbook show how to produce such instructional materials as activity cards, transparencies, books, tapes, slides and multi-media shows.

The purpose of this and other LEARNING Handbooks is to help make teaching and learning more effective, interesting and exciting. Betty Jane Wagner chairs the English/Philosophy Department at the National College of Education. E. Arthur Stunard is Director of Instructional Media at the National College of Education. Their extensive experience has been combined with LEARNING magazine's research facilities and editorial depth to produce this down-to-earth and lively handbook.

Editor: Carol B. Whiteley
Illustrations: Ron Harris
Photography: Jim Collins
Cover: Dennis Ziemienski

Executive Editor: Roberta Suid
Editorial Director: Morton Malkofsky
Design Director: Robert G. Bryant

Copyright © 1976, Education Today Company, Inc., 530 University Avenue, Palo Alto, California 94301. World Rights Reserved. No part of this publication may be reproduced by any mechanical, photographic, or electronic process, or in any other form, nor may it be stored in a retrieval system, transmitted, or otherwise copied for public or private use without prior written permission from Education Today Company, Inc.

Library of Congress Number: 76-29236
International Standard Book Number: 0-915092-10-7

Book Code: 013 • First Printing October 1976

Contents

	Why Bother With Media?	5
Chapter 1	Hands-on Materials	9
Chapter 2	Displays	21
Chapter 3	Multimedia Shows	33
Chapter 4	Lettering	43
Chapter 5	Preserving	51
Chapter 6	Photographing	65
Chapter 7	Movie Making	75
Chapter 8	Making Transparencies	81
	Resources	89

Why Bother With Media?

This book is for beginners. Its first goal is to acquaint you with a wide range of media whose makings are probably available right in your own school. We shall recommend primarily those materials and supplies that are relatively inexpensive.

This goal, however, is just the beginning; our ultimate aim is to help you feel comfortable enough with easy communication-oriented processes to show your students how to use them. This book is a resource for you and your children to use together to explore various ways to prepare, preserve, display and present materials, ideas and projects. We feel these processes can help your students become better learners—more aware of the range of ways they can discover, enjoy and share activities, stories, information and ideas.

MEDIA AND THE CURRICULUM

Media are simply channels through which *any* content is communicated—they are means for both the receiving of and the sending of messages. Since all learning is dependent on this message interchange, any way we can find to enhance and expand the means of communication is going to affect greater learning. Thus, media are appropriate for all curriculum areas. For example, understandings in science or social studies can be mastered more efficiently if concrete experience is meshed with the development of abstract concepts. Demonstrative models, displays, collections, exhibits, mobiles, charts, graphs, maps, films—all can be effective in a number of academic subjects using the processes described in this book.

Media provide a way to enlarge the impact of concrete demonstrations. If change or movement is part of a process you or your children want to present, then a series of time lapse still photos or a movie would be an effective medium. If the information is quantitative, then graphs may work best; if there are several variables, a series of overlays in different colors for an overhead projector would be useful. If a historical drama in costume is part of a social studies unit, try a series of slides accompanied by a taped narrative. To demonstrate mathematics principles, children can make materials such as flip charts, overhead transparencies or felt board manipulatives. They can also make jig saw puzzles, games or flash cards for individual or small group drill.

It is, however, in the mastering of the language arts—speaking, listening, reading, writing and performing—that the use of media is perhaps the most valuable. The full development of a child's language is best assured by small group interaction, and the sharing of projects with the class. Passive reception simply won't do the job. Language itself is nothing other than a medium, one of the means for setting up a relationship among a sender, a receiver and a message. All media share with language common characteristics, and because this is so, communication in one medium is bound to affect one's skill in communicating in another. Learning to compose via media —putting together a slide show, making a series of pictures into a story, showing a set of events through recorded nonverbal sounds— encompasses most of the composition problems we normally associate with verbal composition, and therefore work in the first area should affect and hopefully improve work in the other area.

Another benefit of a child's working with media is a better understanding of everyday electronic media, especially television. One of the best ways for children to become aware of the intent of commercials—strong-impact visual messages—is to mimic them in appropriate media. As children use juxtaposition, subtle connotation and emotional appeal in their own projects, they begin to see them for what they are—means for making a viewer respond as the advertiser wants him to. This awareness is as important in viewing nonverbal messages as in reading printed ones. In either case, critical analysis and a sensitivity to the intent of the sender of a message is as important as understanding the content of a message. All too often, children, who are large-scale consumers of visual and audio information, have little idea how strongly they are influenced by television commercials. Making up their own will let them role-play the producer so when they watch a commercial or show they will do so with a heightened critical awareness of and an appreciation for the potential of the medium of television.

It is not always obvious that when language is the exclusive means of exchanging information, the amount of information available to the learner is inevitably limited. Other media can communicate *more*, not less, than words. For example, to summarize a nonverbal experience in words is much more difficult and limited than to summarize it nonverbally. A purely verbal message calls forth a different, perhaps more limited, kind of attention from its receivers than a nonverbal one does. Each medium, however, has its own potential and limits, and shifting a message from one medium to another is one of the best ways to discover this. The more children experiment with media, the better able they will be to analyze the differences among them.

To answer the question we posed at the beginning of the introduction, we bother with media because they make the information and concepts that are the curriculum come alive and engage the learners, and because they provide a powerful stimulus for the learner's perfection of, review of and communication of what he or she has learned or created. Media then is not a substitute for more traditional means of learning; it is simply another way to develop basic skills.

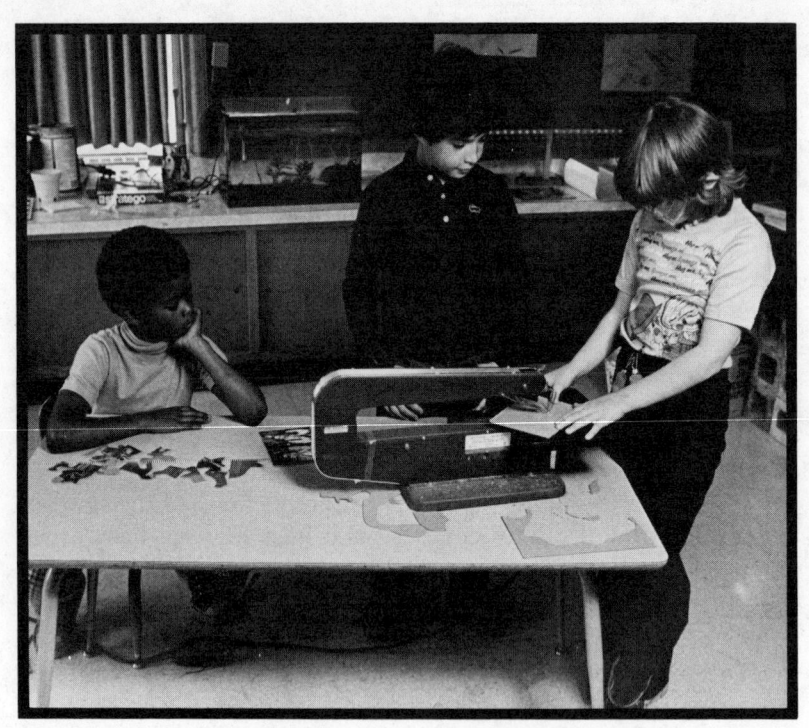

1

Hands-on Materials

Children need materials they can choose among and manipulate—alone or in small groups. In this chapter we shall describe a few of these materials, plus self-made booklets and games.

LAMINATED ACTIVITY CARDS

One of the fastest ways to multiply classroom choices for students is to put directions for alternative activities onto activity cards. Step-by-step procedures can be written and illustrated on both sides of a piece of cardboard, rounded off at the corners and then laminated on both sides.[1] Cards 8½" x 11" are a good size for elementary children because they usually provide enough space for both directions and colorful illustrations. Of course, activity directions can be written on any size card from 3" x 5" on up, but the smaller the card, the less room there is for lively, attention-getting design and illustration.

Activity cards can be displayed using notched wooden holders like this:

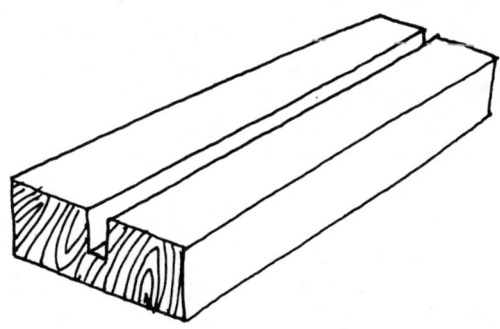

[1]For information on how to laminate, see Chapter 5.

If you want to show a group of activity cards at the same learning station or table, you can stand them vertically in low boxes.

LETTER-MOVING DEVICES

Children who are learning to decode print into speech—that is, who are mastering phonics—can make and play with a variety of letter-moving devices. One such device can be made by cutting two slits in a piece of tagboard with a few letters on it and slipping a paper strip of letters through the slits so that new combinations of letters and thus new words appear. (The letters on the strip should be limited to those the children know.) Both the cardboard and the paper strip can be laminated.[2]

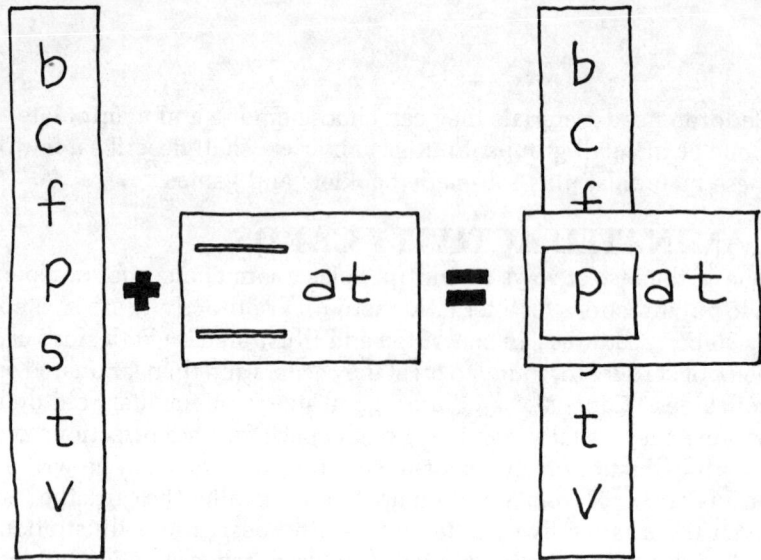

A more versatile device for learning phonics is a word wheel. You can make a word wheel with from two to seven letters. To make a four-letter word wheel, cut two circles of the same size out of cardboard, one for the bottom disk and the other for the top. The circles should be at least 4½" in diameter, although they can be as large as you like. After you cut them out, cut out three smaller circles. If your large circles are 4½" across, the smaller ones should have diameters of 1", 2" and 3", respectively. Cut a window and an arc out of the large circle that will be the top cover of the wheel. The words you make will appear in the window and the open arc will facilitate turning the cardboard circles.

[2]For information on how to laminate, see Chapter 5.

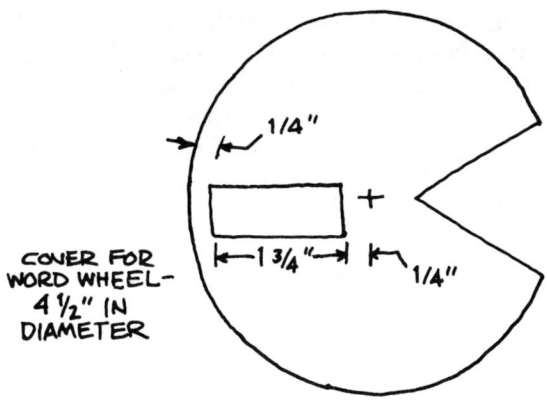

Next, write a number of evenly spaced letters around the edge of each of the other four cardboard disks. If you leave blank spaces in both the largest and smallest circles, this four-letter word wheel will serve also for two- and three-letter words. Be sure to write the letters as they are shown in the next illustration so that those at opposite sides of the disk are upside down from one another. (If children have difficulty correctly writing the letters on the wheels, have them put all five wheels together with a brass fastener in the middle and write their letters through the slot of the top cover wheel—this will help them print all letters in the same direction.) In any case, use the window on the top cover circle as a guide to be sure all the letters on all the circles will be visible through the opening. Make all the letters the same size even though the disks are different sizes.

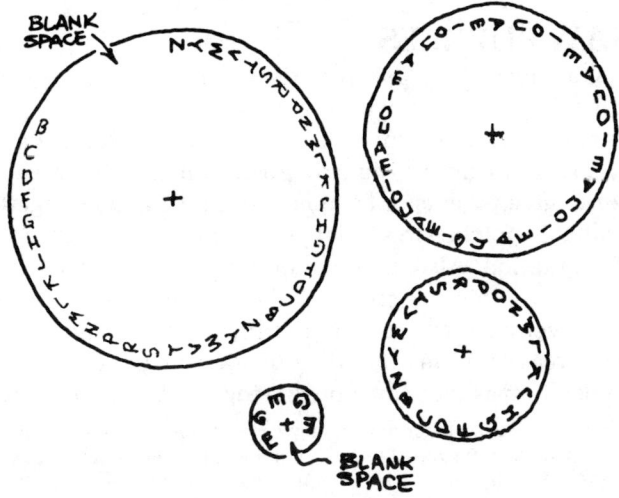

After all the letters are written, you can laminate each disk and then stack them together with the 4½" circle with letters on the bottom, the 3", 2" and 1" circles next and the cover circle on top. When this is done, put a brass fastener through the center, slip a scrap of cardboard under the edge of the top cover sheet to keep the brass fastener from closing so tightly that the five disks cannot rotate freely and then open the brass fastener on the back side of the wheel. The completed wheel should look like this:[3]

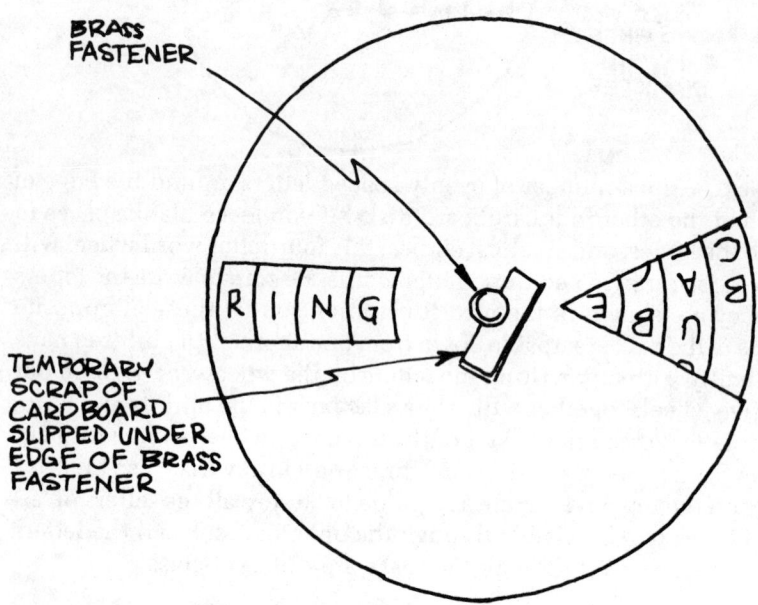

JIG SAW PUZZLES

If you take a few safety precautions, such as wearing goggles and always having an adult working with children, making jig saw puzzles can be a simple and safe process, one with a wide range of educational applications. Jig saw puzzles make attractive gifts for children to give parents or friends, and putting them together provides valuable practice in spatial perception and recognition of pattern configuration. Also, national or continental maps, parts of the body, including internal organs and bones, geometric shapes, etc., can be converted into puzzles, cutting along boundaries of geographical areas or around the edges of other shapes so students learn relative position as they put a puzzle together. Materials for drill or

[3] For more information on letter-moving devices and how they can be used, see James Moffett and Betty Jane Wagner, *Student-Centered Language Arts and Reading* (Boston: Houghton Mifflin, 1976).

review for word recognition, spelling, grammar, math, social studies or science also can be put into a jig saw puzzle form.

Recommended Materials
- A vibrating jig saw
  You may be able to borrow one from the industrial arts department of your school, or you can buy one at a large hardware or discount store.
- Extra jig saw blades
  These are inexpensive; keep a supply of extras because they do occasionally break under continual use.
- Chipboard (approximately 1/16" thick) or other heavy card stock Masonite or plywood can also be used.
- A picture from a magazine, old book, postcard, etc., a map, math problem, sentence or original drawing to make into a puzzle
- Dry mounting tissue or rubber cement
- Laminating film, either the hot press type or Contact shelf paper
- Hot press[4] or household iron or rubber cement
- Other dry mounting tools, such as a tacking iron, flexible steel ruler, razor blades and holder, paper cutter, cutting board, pencil, etc.[5]
- Manilla envelope or box in which to store the finished puzzle
- Fine flint sandpaper, available at a hardware store (optional)

Procedure
1. Rough cut the picture, map, photo or other visual so it is slightly larger than the desired finishing size, matching it to the card stock on which it is to be mounted.
2. Glue, preferably with a hot press, the visual to the top surface of the card stock.
3. Laminate the mounted visual to protect its top surface; hot press lamination of both sides is best.
4. Now trim the mounted and laminated visual to the desired size using scissors, a razor blade, paper cutter or the jig saw.
5. Make sure that the cutting blade teeth on the jig saw blade are pointed downward toward the table. Then begin cutting the picture (puzzle) into pieces of varying shapes and sizes. The size of the pieces will probably be in reverse proportion to the age of the puzzle maker; the smaller the pieces, the greater the challenge. Be sure the puzzle lies flat on the table as it is being pushed toward the blade.
6. Depending on the materials used, you may need to touch up or sand with fine-grade flint sandpaper any rough edges that remain.

[4]For information on hot presses, see Chapter 5.
[5]Turn to Chapter 5 for details on the materials needed and the procedure for mounting and laminating.

Do this lightly so the puzzle pieces will still lock together tightly.

SELF-MADE BOOKLETS
Flip Movies
To make a flip movie, you'll need a number of sheets of typing paper (or any thin white paper) cut in 3½" squares. On the first sheet, draw a picture of a person, animal or object that is capable of motion. (Stick figures are easy to start with; drawing with colored felt markers creates high-contrast pictures quickly.) Next, put a clean sheet of paper on top of the picture and paper clip the two together. Put the two sheets up against a window pane and trace the first figure onto the top sheet, changing the figure slightly. Now, take another clean sheet and clip it to the last picture you have drawn, removing the first picture and setting it aside. Again, trace the picture, changing it slightly, and then continue the process until you have finished showing all the action you want to have in your movie. Always use the most recently drawn picture as a model for the next, and number each picture so you can keep them in order.

When the flip movie is completed, it should be stapled along the top or side edge. When someone flips through the pages he'll see such things as a chick hatching from an egg, a grandfather clock ticking or a clown falling off a skateboard. The effect is that of an animated movie and provides good practice for making a real 8 mm. animated film.[6]

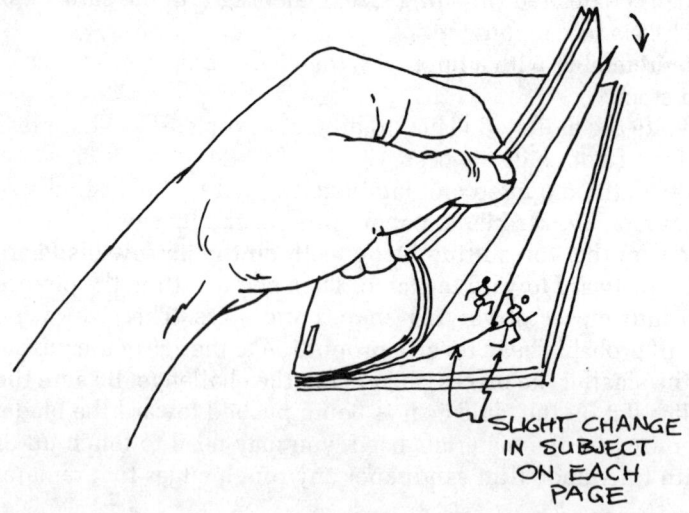

SLIGHT CHANGE IN SUBJECT ON EACH PAGE

[6]See Chapter 7 to learn about animation.

In conjunction with this activity you can show your children how a 16 mm. film is actually a series of still pictures just like flip books. Holding some 16 mm. film up to the light, explain that when the film goes quickly through the projector, it makes the characters seem to move just as the figures seem to move on pages that are flipped in rapid succession.

Bound Books
Very young children can easily make booklets with covers of construction paper or tagboard fastened together with staples, paper-holding rivets, brads, yarn or string threaded through punched holes. A much more satisfying product, however, is the bound book, one well worth the extra effort and one that even young children can master.
A SIMPLE PROCESS
Materials and Equipment
- 1/16"-thick chipboard or railroad board, which can be purchased at an art supply or printer's supply store, or cardboard
- 2"-wide cloth tape (Mystik tape)
- Wallpaper sample book, usually available free from a paint and wallpaper store; Contact paper or scraps of cloth material
- Rubber cement
- Paper cutter, heavy scissors, x-acto knife or razor blade for cutting cardboard
- Heavy-duty stapler
- Paper or particular pages to be bound

Procedure
1. Cut two pieces of cardboard ½" longer and ¼" wider than the pages to be bound. These will become the top and bottom covers of the book.

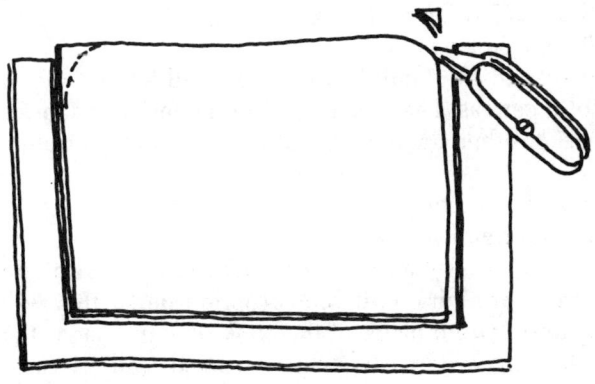

2. Cut a ¾" strip off the top and bottom covers along the edge where the paper of the book will be fastened together.
3. Cover both sides of the large pieces of cardboard with Contact paper, or glue on wallpaper or cloth with rubber cement.
4. Lay the large and small pieces of cardboard side by side, leaving approximately 1/16" between them. Then fasten them together with a strip of cloth tape. Turn the joined cardboard over and do the same on the other side. Repeat for the back cover.
5. Put the pages of the book flush with the edges of the small strips of the cardboard cover that are now taped to the rest of the cover. Staple the pages to the cover like this:

Now the book will open at the taped hinges.
6. For a more finished look, cover the stapled edge with another piece of cloth tape.

A MORE SPECTACULAR PROCESS
Materials and Equipment
- Two pieces of 1/16" chipboard or railroad board
- Sailcloth, canvas, heavy cotton duck material or fabric scraps
- Fotoflat[7] or other dry mounting tissue, available at photo supply stores
- An electric household iron or a hot press
- Hammer and nail or awl
- Paper cutter, heavy scissors, x-acto knife or razor blade
- Two sheets of high-quality construction paper that will become the top and bottom pages of the book plus the pages to be bound
- Large darning needle and heavy carpet thread

[7]For information on Fotoflat, see Chapter 5.

Procedure
1. There are two ways to sew a book together. (In either case the top and bottom pages of the book are glued to the inside of the top and bottom covers.) One way is to fold the pages in the middle and make an uneven number of holes (with hammer and nail or awl) along the fold for sewing. Another way is to cut the pages separately and stack them together evenly. Then iron a white binding strip (sold at art stores) over the edge, covering approximately ¾" of the first and last pages of the stack as well as the back edge of all the pages. On this strip draw a guideline about a half inch from the edge and make an odd number of holes along it.

2. Leaving enough extra thread for tying, start sewing the pages together by poking the needle through the middle hole, then back up one of the holes next to it and on to the end of the page. Then sew down to the middle through the same holes. Continue sewing to the other end of the page and back to the middle. Tie the thread that is left to the thread you left hanging from the middle hole. Here is the path the thread should follow:

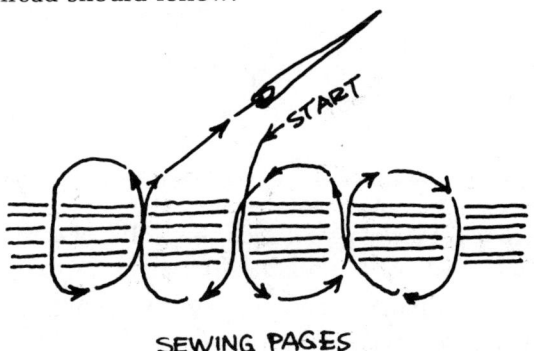

SEWING PAGES

3. Cut two pieces of cardboard ½" longer and ¼" wider than the pages to be bound.
4. Lay out the fabric with the pattern side down. Set the cardboard pieces side by side on the cloth, leaving about ¾" between the two pieces if the book is to have approximately 40 pages and leaving less space in between if the book is to be thinner. Cut the material so it extends approximately 1" beyond the perimeter of the cardboard pieces.

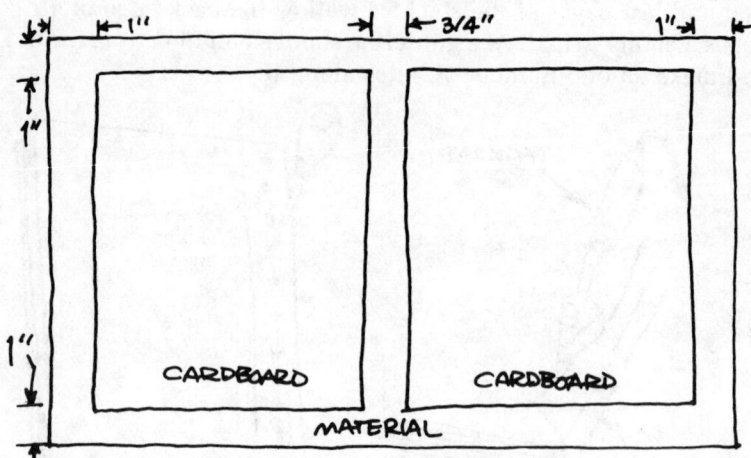

5. Remove the cardboard pieces and put dry mounting tissue (preferably Fotoflat) over all of the cloth. Then replace the cardboard.
6. Trim the corners of the cloth, leaving at least ½" to turn over each corner.

7. Fold the edges of the material and the Fotoflat over the cardboard and glue them down with a regular iron or a tacking iron.[8]
8. Put a piece of dry mounting tissue on top of the two pieces of card-

[8] See Chapter 5 for an illustration of the dry mounting process.

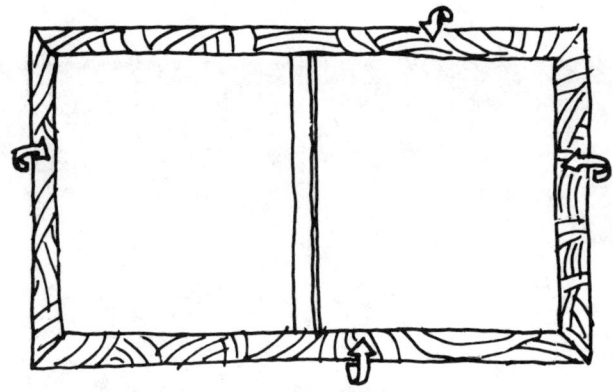

board and attach this to the end sheets (the two pieces of construction paper).

Binding a book or pieces of information in a permanent form provides a powerful stimulus not only for writing but for proofreading and editing to perfect a composition before making it into a book. Some librarians have encouraged young authors by putting call numbers on their bound books and shelving them with the school library collection. There is great interest and excitement in finding one's own name in the library's card catalogue.[9]

GAMES

Making card and board games can hold as much fascination for children as playing them. Laminating[10] the playing boards, cardboard playing pieces and decks of cards not only increases their life but also makes them look and feel more like their commercial counterparts. You and your children can design quiz games that fit almost any curriculum, lettering the playing pieces onto cardboard and then laminating them.[11]

Most games children play possess an element of uncertainty or chance. One way to assure this feature is to play games that involve the vagaries of a spinner. To make a simple spinner, attach a metal arrow (these can be bought at most teacher supply stores or teacher centers) with a grommet to the center of a circle cut from heavy cardboard. If you cannot find a metal arrow, use a cardboard one and attach it loosely with a brass fastener.

---

[9] For more ideas in this area, see *How to Make Your Own Books* by Harvey Weiss (New York: T. Y. Crowell, 1974).
[10] For information on how to laminate, see Chapter 5.
[11] See the LEARNING Handbook by Craig Pearson and Joseph Marfuggi, *Creating and Using Learning Games*; and for ideas on how children can develop imaginative board games that go beyond mere strategy into storytelling, see Herbert R. Kohl, *Math, Writing and Games in the Open Classroom* (New York: Random House, 1974).

2
Displays

The following projects can provide you with a number of easy-to-make display items.

CHARTS THAT MOVE
Clothespin Match-up
Laminated[1] charts made of heavy cardboard can invite learner response by being paired with a set of flat-sided clothespins with words or figures on them. The clothespin that names the picture on the chart is attached to the chart at the appropriate spot. Here is how a compound word recognition chart for a primary classroom might look:

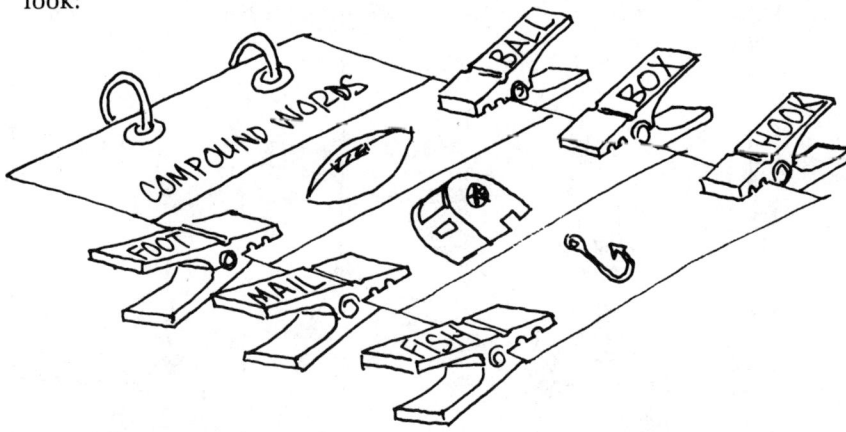

[1]For information on how to laminate, see Chapter 5.

Flip Chart

A flip chart is simply a set of poster board cards of equal size hinged at the top. If grommets are attached along the top and metal rings inserted through them, a set of flip chart cards is fairly permanent, easy to handle and useful for any sequenced presentation of information. Each card can end with an exercise or question that the user works out or answers before he flips the card over to the next page to find out if he is right.

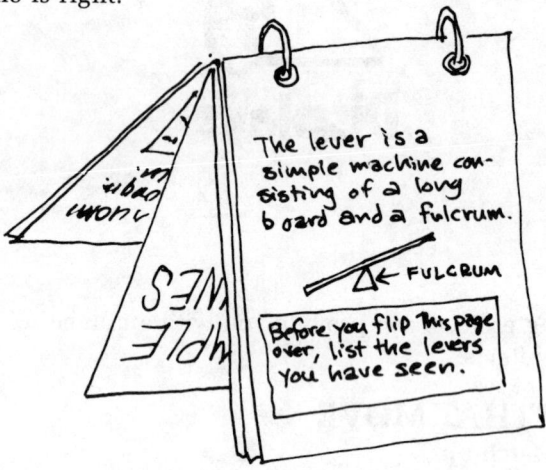

   To add grommets you will need a grommet kit, which you can buy from a hardware store or a sailboat equipment shop. In the grommet kit is a hole cutter, a die top and a base and a set of grommets. (Choose a kit with grommets appropriate to the size of your cards.) Wherever you want a hole, place the cutter over the poster board and a wooden block below it and strike the cutter with a mallet or hammer.

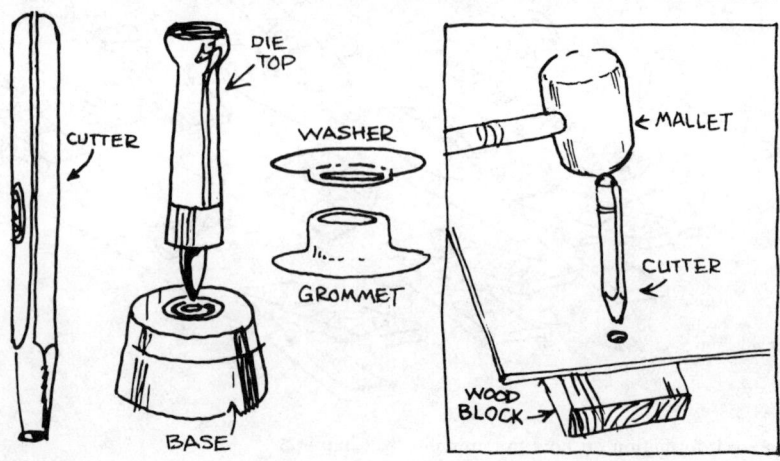

22

Then insert a grommet from the bottom side of the poster board, placing the grommet on the base that comes with the kit so that it fits into the hole on the base.

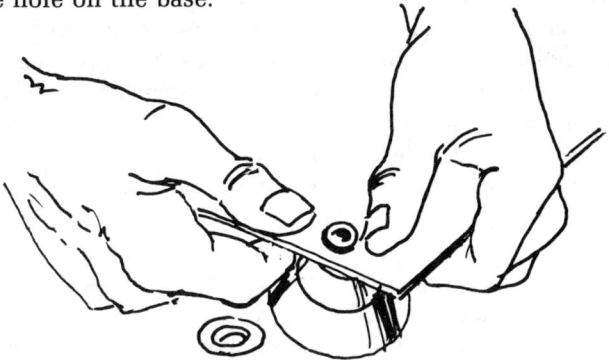

Next, put a washer, with the rounded side up, on top of the poster board where the grommet is sticking through. Insert the die top into the hole—

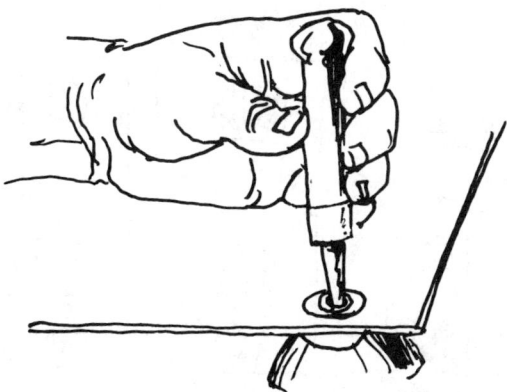

tap it with a mallet, lightly at first, and then more firmly until the grommet is set.

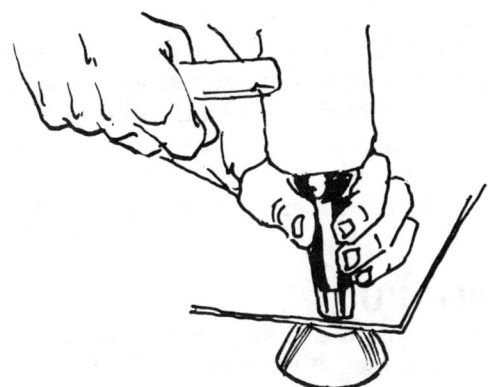

Pocket Chart
A wall chart with sturdy commercial or homemade envelopes stapled to it is an old stand-by display in kindergarten and primary classrooms, useful for a variety of purposes. One use is helping children learn to spell and recognize their name. Each pocket of the display can have a child's name written on it. A nearby table can be covered with small cards, each card having one child's name on it. As each child enters the room he can find the card with his name on it and put it into the matching pocket on the wall chart. Children will quickly learn to recognize their own names and match them, and before long they can begin to help each other as well.

Pocket charts are also useful for showing the place value of numbers or for phonics drill. Children can cut out pictures from magazines and "file" them in the chart pockets according to their initial sounds.

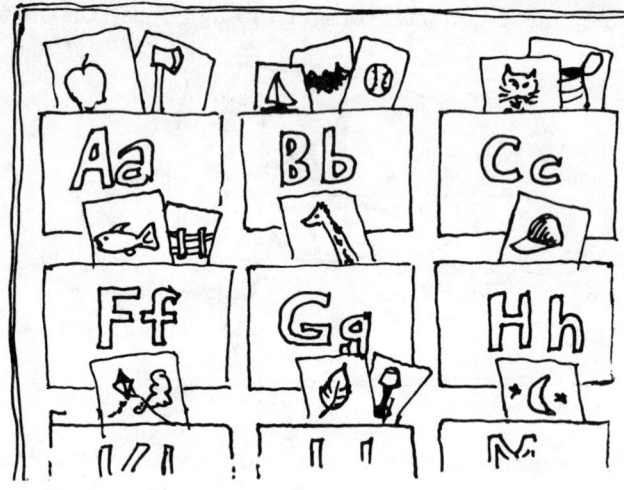

Older children can file word cards according to parts of speech or can use pocket charts as story starters, putting all the ideas for characters in the "Who" pocket, settings for a story (the more unusual, the better) in a "Where" pocket and problems characters might face in a "What" pocket. Then each student can randomly select one of each and build a story around it, making sure the character, place and problem he has gotten from the pocket chart appear somewhere in the story.

FELT BOARD
A felt board is simply a piece of plywood covered with felt to which objects glued to a sensitive backing will adhere. This type of display .

can be made quickly; objects to place on it generally are easy to design and manipulate.

Materials Needed
- A piece of plywood or lightweight wallboard 24" x 36" x at least ⅜"
- A piece of felt large enough to cover and lap over the edges of the board
  Wool rather than synthetic felt material is much preferred, but is more costly and hard to find. Material that is 50% wool and 50% rayon felt is more common and cheaper; suede, duvetyn or velour with the fuzzy side out also works well; cotton flannel is less effective but much cheaper.
- A heavy-duty staple gun with ¼" staples
- Heavy-duty scissors designed to cut material such as felt
- Cardboard for manipulatives
- Strips of felt or flannel, or open-kote garnet #80 grit sandpaper, available at most hardware stores, to glue onto the backs of manipulatives

Procedure
1. On a sturdy table or the floor, center the plywood on the piece of felt. Cut away approximately ¾" from each corner of the plywood.

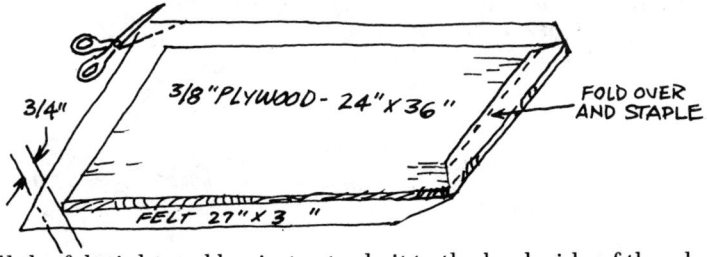

2. Pull the felt tight and begin to staple it to the back side of the plywood.
3. As the stapling continues, be sure to pull the felt tightly across the front of the board. Loose or sagging felt will not provide a good surface for the manipulatives.
4. A simple stand can be attached to the board. It might be another smaller piece of plywood hinged at the top of the back of the felt board and attached at the bottom with a chain or heavy cord.

25

5. If you prefer, you can reinforce the back of one long side of the board with a 1"-thick strip of lumber. Then you can attach screw eyes along the edge of this board so the felt board can be hung from cup hooks placed along the top edge of a chalk board or other molding.
6. Children's drawings or pictures from magazines or old books, glued on tagboard, can be glued onto a backing of fabric, preferably felt, and then trimmed. To do this, follow the directions in Chapter 5 for "Rubber Cement Mounting," substituting a piece of felt slightly larger than the picture for the card stock backing and using rubber cement or Fotoflat as mounting tissue. Press the picture and the felt in a hot press for approximately one minute at 180°F. If you want to laminate the manipulatives, follow the directions for laminating in Chapter 5. Glue heavy manipulatives onto sandpaper instead of felt to keep them from slipping on the felt board. When cutting or trimming sandpaper, use an old pair of scissors that you consider expendable.

Individual Felt Boards

You can make this display and storage unit out of a cigar box, reinforcing the paper that is used to hinge the cover with two tiny metal hinges. The top of the box can be covered with felt or other material and cutouts or materials can be stored inside.

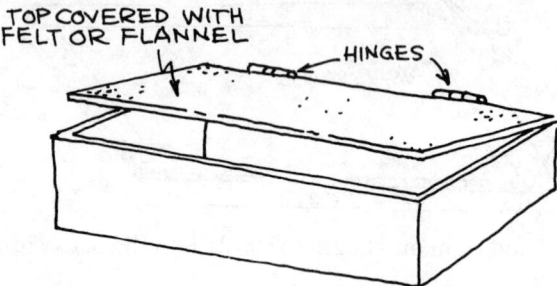

Cutouts might be letters of the alphabet for making words, circle segments to match with fractions or geometric shapes such as these to illustrate concepts.

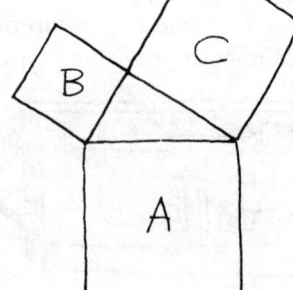

Whether large or individual, felt boards can be used to show any objects that change relative position.

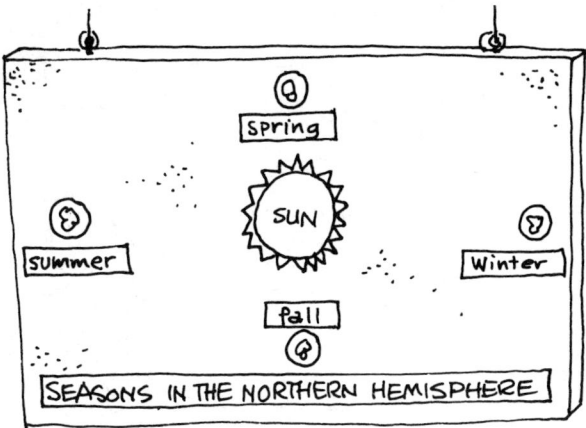

Felt boards can also be used as a way to stage remembered or original stories. Characters and scenery can be drawn onto cardboard, glued to a backing, trimmed and then moved about on the felt board as the story is told.

HANGING DISPLAYS

Once you find yourself committed to displaying student-produced projects, a problem usually arises: Where do I put them up? After bulletin boards and backs of bookcases and study carrels are plastered with children's art, reports or hands-on charts, you may decide to start hanging things from the ceiling. The easiest way to do this is to fasten large screw eyes to the ceiling and thread clothesline through them. By putting each screw about a yard from the walls in each of the corners of the room, you can deftly net yourself a roomful of eye-catching display space. If children's work is mounted on heavy cardboard and hung from a string clipped to the clothesline with a clothespin, it will be low enough for kids to read and will turn so both sides can be examined.

Box Mobile
If you want to display five sides of a project at once, make box mobiles and hang these from the clothesline set-up just described. Take six sheets of construction paper and either write or draw with a felt pen or glue illustrations or reports onto all but one of these sheets. The blank one will be the top of the box. Fasten a string to the middle of that sheet either by knotting one end of the string and poking the other end through a small hole or by stapling the string to the paper.

Then staple the six sheets to form a three-dimensional box and hang the box from the clothesline with the attached string.

Hanger Display
Another simple display that can be made is a clothes hanger mobile. A set of reports that are written onto cards can be attached with string to the bottom of a hanger. A drawing or diagram can be put on the back of each card. Then the hanger can be hung on the clothesline.

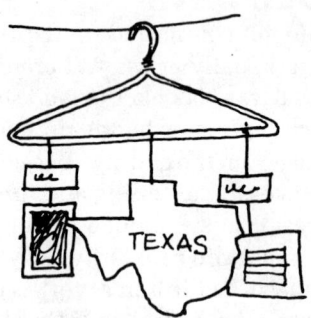

Clothes hanger mobiles work well for science or social studies reports. For example, each child can take a different state or country and on a separate card put the climate, government, natural resources, major cities, history, arts, etc.; or each child can report on a different reptile, describing on separate cards its life cycle, habitat, food, natural enemies and so on.

Mailing Tube
For this display you'll need a mailing tube or the tube from a roll of paper towels, three poster boards, all the same size, glue and string. First, cut with an x-acto knife or a razor blade three narrow vertical

slots in the mailing tube; each should be the length of the short end of the three poster boards. Space the slots equally around the tube. Draw or mount the material to be displayed in sequence on the front and back sides of the poster boards, laminating them as well (see Chapter 5), if you like. Then put casein glue, such as Elmer's, on both sides of the poster board and around the edges of one of the vertical slots. Insert this glued side into the slot; insert the others in proper sequence so the six posters can be viewed in order by turning the display around. To strengthen it, thread string through holes at the top outside edge of the cards. Hang the mailing tube mobile by knotting one end of a piece of string and punching the other end through a hole on one side of the tube near the top; then punch another hole opposite the first one on the other side of the tube, thread the string through it and tie another knot on the inside. Tie another string to the middle of the first one and clip the free end to the clothesline.

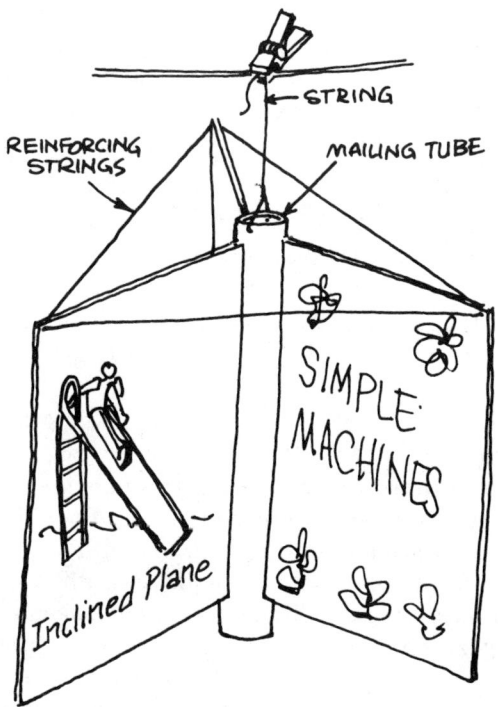

ENLARGEMENTS

Any projector can be used to make enlargements. Simply place it far enough away from a large piece of newsprint, poster board or tagboard to project an image the size you need. You can project maps, pictures of insects in various stages of metamorphosis, leaves, charts, diagrams, profiles of class members or whatever and trace around the outline, taking care to keep your head below your felt pen or pencil so you don't shadow the area you are tracing.

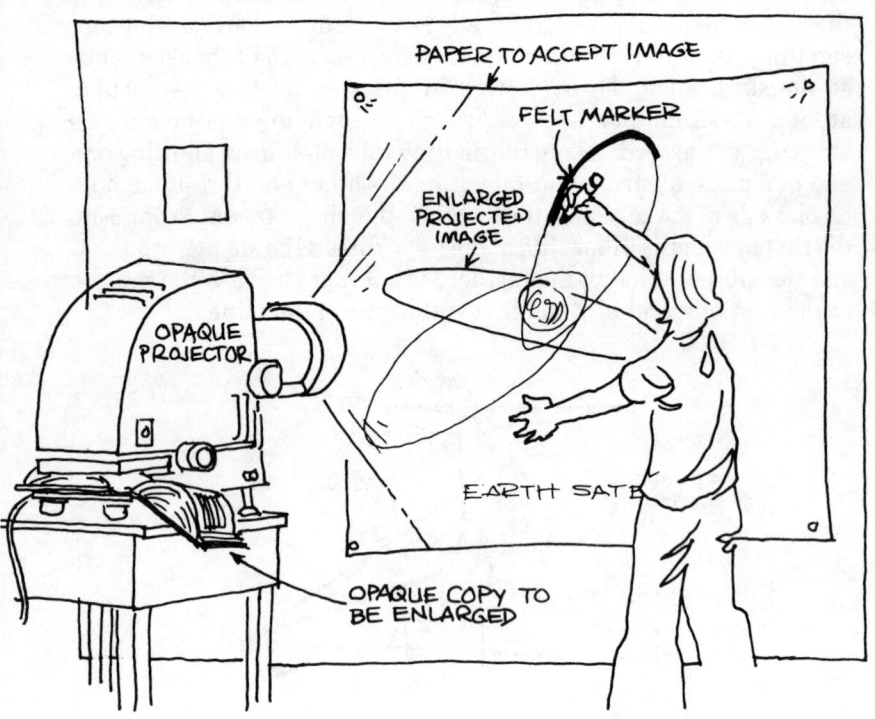

If you want an outline to use for painting scenery for a drama, simply project a sketch, drawing or other picture of the objects you need onto wallboard, trace around the outline and then paint it in.

Although opaque projectors are bulky and difficult to use compared to overheads, the new higher output opaque machines project book or magazine pictures or children's drawings clearly onto a screen if you use them in a completely darkened room. The biggest advantages of the opaque projector are that you can work directly with original artwork and do not need to make transparencies or slides beforehand, and that you can learn to operate them quickly.

For illustration, here is how you might produce a cloth hanging in the style of the embroidered linen Bayeaux Tapestry to accompany the study of the Middle Ages, including the invasion of England in

1066 by William the Conqueror. First, look carefully at pictures of the actual tapestry[2] and select a section to use. Then make a drawing of this section and enlarge it by projecting it through an opaque projector onto white fabric, such as a sheet, and draw around the images with wax crayon. Color in the enlarged picture with wax crayons and finally iron the wall hanging (if it's on a sheet or fabric) from the back to set the color. You can do this by putting the picture face down on a piece of brown paper and then ironing it.

[2]Excellent reproductions can be found in Norman Denny and Josephine Filmer-Sankey, *The Bayeaux Tapestry: The Story of the Norman Conquest 1066* (New York: Atheneum, 1966).

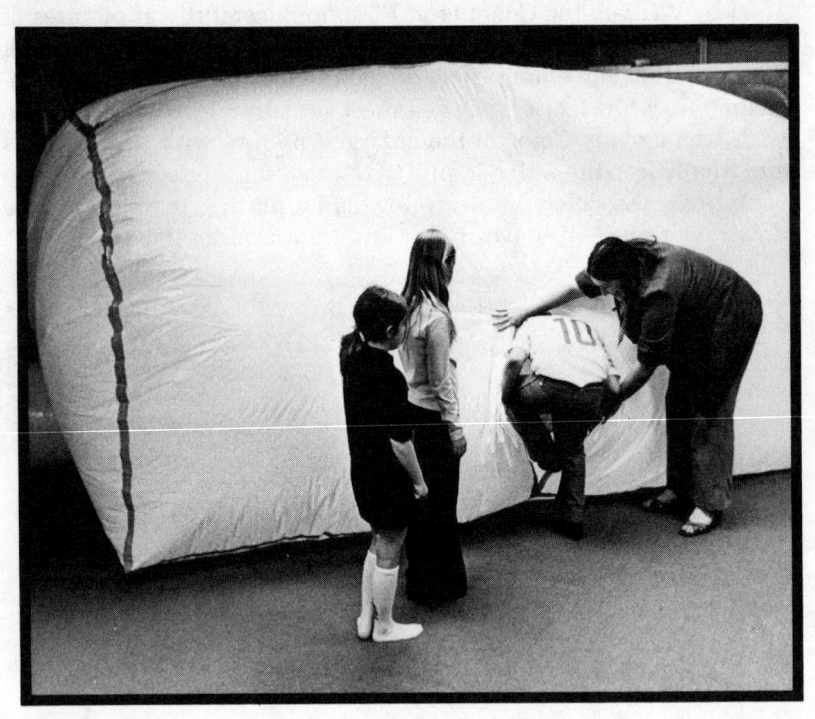

3
Multimedia Shows

By talking along with projected shows or combining various projecting and audio techniques, children can present their versions of material they have read, share original stories or pass on information to their classmates in a highly arresting and effective way. Here are just a few suggestions for producing multimedia shows.

AN OATMEAL BOX PLANETARIUM
An inexpensive way to project patterns of light to illustrate a specific constellation is to make a mini-planetarium out of an oatmeal box and a flashlight. To do this, draw a circle on the bottom of an empty oatmeal box, making it just the size of the back end of an ordinary home flashlight; cut out this circle. Then lower the flashlight backwards into the box so it goes through the hole up to the larger front end behind the reflector. Now, using black Mystic or electrical tape, seal up the opening around the flashlight so no light can get through. You may prefer to stuff cotton or scraps of material such as felt into the crack between the cardboard and the flashlight. The important thing is to be sure no light can leak out around the opening.

Take the top off the oatmeal box and lay it upside down on a cutting board or other surface that can take the abuse of having holes poked in it. On the inside of the cover put pencil dots in the same relative position as the stars are in the constellation you have chosen to project. When all the dots are plotted, poke through them using a needle. Vary the size of the holes according to the brightness of the stars.

Now, put the top on the oatmeal box and go into a dark closet or other small room. Turn on your flashlight and project the constellation, moving it around until it is in the same relative position in the "sky" as the real constellation. (After you have shown your class how to make the planetariums, all the children can project their constellations at once, moving them around until each is in its proper location in the "sky." Then, using the Little Dipper as a guide, the kids can wheel all the constellations slowly westward, just as the real constellations do every night. The child with the Little Dipper can use the North Star—the last one in the Dipper's handle—as a pivot, twisting his flashlight slowly to the left so the bowl of his Dipper swings around its handle. The other children can try to keep their constellations in the same relative position to the Little Dipper, moving at the same pace, each making a large circle with his oatmeal box.)

OPAQUE AND OVERHEAD SHOWS

Opaque projectors are particularly convenient for stimulating oral composition by young children because all they need do is draw a series of pictures to illustrate a story they have made up or recall and then tell that story as they show the pictures in sequence. They can give oral reports on a text they have read by simply showing the class the sequence of pictures in the book, using the pictures as stimuli to their memory as they recall the material they have read earlier.

A wide variety of shows and demonstrations can be created via the overhead projector. For example, iron filings can be spread on the surface of an overhead and a magnet can be used to create a magnetic field that is simultaneously projected. Simple Centigrade and Fahrenheit thermometers can be cut out of card stock with a window in each and taped side by side on a piece of acetate, adding the calibrations at the side of each with a fine-point felt-tipped pen. If letters are at least ⅜" high, they will project well. A translucent strip of red plexiglass (a plastic glass-like polymer available from many lumber or hardware suppliers) can be put over each thermometer to show how the same temperature is registered differently on each scale.

A transparent clock can also be cut from plexiglass—opaque gummed-back numbers[1] and moveable cardboard hands can be glued on and then projected to practice telling time. Tools such as transparent protractors or rulers can be projected and their features and uses demonstrated to a large group. Presentations using overlays of various colors are ideal for showing changes in a map throughout a historical period or for showing the different layers—bone structure, internal organs, muscles, nerves and epidermis—of an animal or a

[1]See Chapter 4.

man. Overlays can be made quickly by using wide-tipped felt pens.[2]

Opaque cardboard puppets are effective for shadow plays projected via the overhead. To make it possible for an off-stage puppeteer to move a cutout puppet without being seen, attach a strip of clear x-ray film as a handle. The projected image will be only the silhouetted figure moving across the screen. Translucent scenery can be painted on a transparency to serve as background for the scenes of the puppet show.

Children can create different moods by presenting abstract images or moving designs such as geometric shapes, cutout snowflakes attached to strips of transparent x-ray film or transparencies in several colors with different grids or designs that are moved to create varied patterns. Shadows of dancing fingers or hands have a mesmerizing effect. Abstract shows of this sort combine well with recorded music. For a capricious mood show, make an envelope out of x-ray film, taping the sides securely with Scotch or Mystik tape, and fill it partially with liquid shampoo or vegetable oil. Then add food coloring and various small opaque flat objects such as cardboard cutouts, tiddledywinks, sand or paper clips, and tape up the top. Put this envelope on top of the overhead and press it in various places to create a moving image.

SLIDE-TAPE SHOWS

Selecting and ordering a set of slides and then adding an oral or taped narration or music is a good learning experience, one entailing observation, differentiation, recognition of similarities and pattern and the pulling together of something into one coherent whole. Begin either by taking pictures for the slide show or by choosing among commercially produced slides. (These may be found among rejected slides in school or home collections.) Try to choose pictures that relate to a specific theme. (When children make slide shows you can help them see what they have collected by saying, "You seem to like the way trees look early or late in the day," or "Most of the animals in your set of slides seem to be very young," or "You have picked out some ugly things in your neighborhood, haven't you? What could you say in a commentary about all of these things?") When the slides are collected, they should be shown in such a way that one clear thesis is presented. A narrative along with the show can be a valuable exercise in oral composition.

Student-made slides (see the following section) are appropriate for projected autobiographies, original stories (sometimes calling for subjects dressed in costume), "definitions" of emotional words

[2]For information on how to make transparencies, see Chapter 8.

like "love," "pollution," or "wonder," documentaries of news events in the school or community, information about classroom pets or other science projects, or poems. A live or taped narrative can accompany the slide show. If your goal is to provide a student-centered goal for writing, have the child write a carefully edited script to read as he shows the slides. A taped musical background might be played as an accompaniment to a live narrative to help establish mood or pace of presentation. The best background music does not have words nor an easily recognized tune.

SLIDE-MAKING WITHOUT A CAMERA

One of the easiest and cheapest ways to make slides is to select frames you want from damaged or outdated filmstrips, cut them apart and insert them in slide mounts. These mounts can be bought at most camera supply centers. For filmstrip frames you will need 35 mm. half-frame slide mounts.[3]

Inexpensive slides can also be made by the color lifting process described in Chapter 8. You can either lift the ink from a small picture or from a portion of a larger one, provided it is printed on clay-coated paper. Then you fit the transparency into either a half- or a full-frame 35 mm. 2" x 2" mount. Tape the transparency in place with frosted Mylar tape, sealing it on all four sides. Once mounted, spray the dull side with clear plastic spray to protect the ink surface you just removed from the paper and to make the slide more transparent.

Children who can write or draw tiny characters may find making their own slides or filmstrips challenging. They simply draw directly onto a specially treated blank film, called "U" film, which is then inserted into a projector for viewing. All the materials you need for making full-color slides or filmstrips without a camera can be found in the "U" Film Filmstrip Kit.[4]

CASSETTE RECORDINGS

Because of its convenience, ease of operation and low cost, the audio cassette recorder is excellent for slide-tape shows as well as for interviews, reports, stories, book reviews, group discussions to listen to and evaluate later, radio programs, choral readings, songs, etc. This portable recorder is especially handy for compiling a tape to be used as an audio-association guessing game. You simply record onto a

---

[3]To facilitate viewing filmstrips, you can buy a plastic filmstrip viewer with a built-in magnifying glass.

[4]This can be ordered from Prima Education Products, 2 S. Buckhout St., Irvington-on-Hudson, N.Y. 10533.

tape a series of sounds, such as a car door slamming, a car motor starting, a dog's bark or the screech of brakes, and ask class members to tell what they hear when the tape is played back. By connecting a tape recorder to a phonograph as described below you can transfer selected sounds from one of the many good sound effects records in a sequence that tells a story and have the class guess what is happening. They might improvise a drama or write a story to go along with the recorded sounds. Most cassette models have become fairly standardized, so if you can operate one, you can probably run any kind. Ideally, a machine should include both an auxiliary input and output, which will allow you to transfer sound from one machine to another without specially designed patching cables. With an auxiliary input and output, all you need do to dub another tape of high quality from one cassette to another is to match auxiliary or line output to auxiliary or line input and connect these with a suitable patch cord.

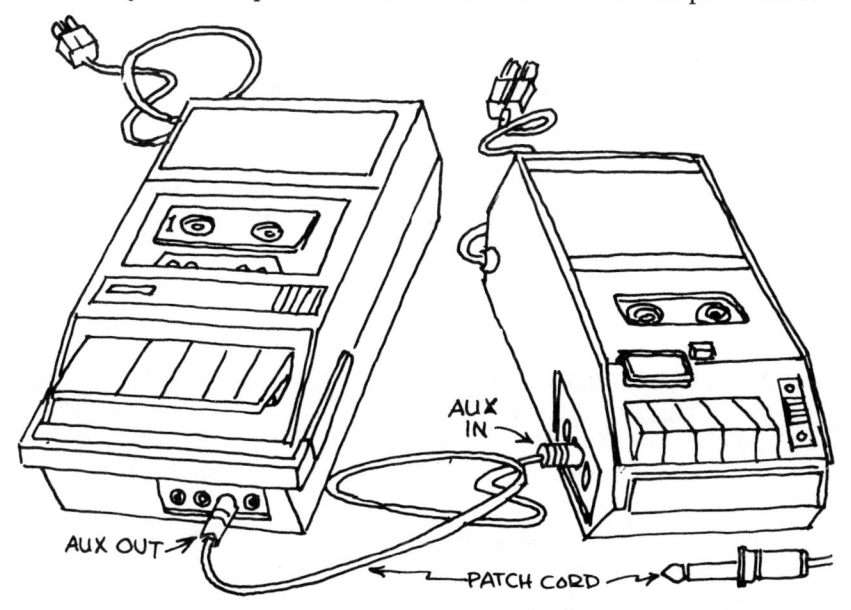

As long as you can match AUX-OUT to AUX-IN, you can dub not only from one cassette to another, but also from a reel-to-reel recorder to a cassette, or from a phonograph to a cassette.

If you are using inexpensive recorders that do not have auxiliary input and output capability, you can still transfer the recording by using an inexpensive special matching-type patch cord, available through your local A-V supplier. With this cord you connect the speaker or monitor output of one recorder with the microphone input of another one. Almost all recorders are able to do this. But without using the special patch cord, you are unlikely to get a sound transfer, or, if you do, there will be an audio hum that will distort the quality of the tape.

Cassettes are easy to find and many are inexpensive. All standard cassettes are the same size, but therein lies a problem. The longer the recording time on a single cassette, the thinner the tape must be to fit into the cassette. Thus C-90 (tapes with 90 minutes of recording time) and C-120 (tapes with 120 minutes of recording time) tapes may be convenient since they don't have to be changed as often as the C-30, C-45 or C-60 tapes, but they are not as strong and thus break more easily. For school purposes it is usually better to use a medium- to high-quality cassette of a 60-minute or less length. If you have a cassette you want to keep and continue to use, rather than erase and record over again, you can prevent accidental erasure by removing the tab at the back edge of the cassette.

MOVIES

If you haven't the money to make your own movies with a camera[5], you can still put together a movie collage, splicing bits of old, discarded movie film into a sequence of your own choosing. Television stations regularly discard hundreds of feet of used news or commercial film footage; ask your local station to give some to you. Businesses or libraries also discard old film they no longer need for advertising or education purposes. Your district's instructional media center also may be a source of supply.

After you gather several pieces of old film, you can view them, select portions you like and then edit them into your own film. New juxtapositions of old film footage are often comic. If the sound is turned off when the edited film is projected, you can add your own live or taped narration to enhance or change the intent of the footage.

To splice a movie film, you can use a movie repair kit, available at large photo supply stores. You will also need splicing tape.

Another way to make instant camera-less movies is to draw with a felt marker onto a clear leader (the blank tape at the beginning of a film) or scratch out a pattern onto a black leader. You can buy inexpensive reclaimed 16 mm. clear film from a 16 mm. supply outlet.[6] You can either put wiggling designs all along the film, or you can put one tiny figure into each space between the sprocket holes, creating animation the same way you do for flip movies.[7]

[5]For more on movie making, see Chapter 7.
[6]Two such suppliers are SOS Photo-Cine-Optics, Inc., 315 W. 43rd St., New York, N.Y. 10036; and Hollywood Film Company, 256 N. Seward St., Hollywood, Ca. 90038.
[7]For more on making flip movies, see Chapter 1.

A REAR-VIEW PROJECTION SCREEN

The possibilities for multimedia presentations are increased if the image to be presented is projected from behind a screen. If the screen is large enough, it can also serve for shadow plays or for combined projections and shadow shows that feature live actors. For example, a picture of a Valley Forge encampment might be projected from behind onto a large rear-view screen, and between the screen and the projector a student dressed in a sentry costume, holding a toy shotgun, might be silhouetted. As this is enacted, another classmate can read or tell the story to go with the image.

   To make an inexpensive rear-view projection screen, fasten together four 2" x 2" boards of any length you like using metal corner braces. If you want to be able to prop up the screen on the backs of two chairs, leave an extra length of board extending beyond each of the two top corners.

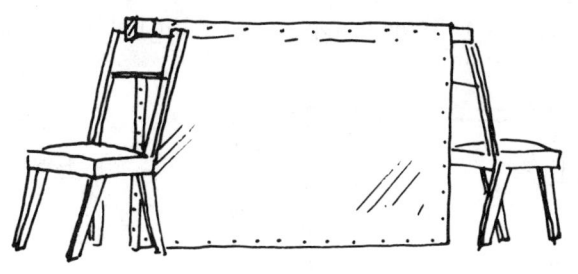

   Then thumbtack or staple with a heavy staple gun a translucent, not transparent, plastic drop cloth or old bed sheet around the edges of the frame. This creates a screen that can be used either for rear-view or front-view projection.

A MEDIA BUBBLE

A media bubble is simply a large, translucent tent that functions as a screen for several simultaneously projected shows. You crawl inside to view the various images that are projected onto the walls and to listen to the tape that goes with them.

A media bubble is easy to build.

Materials
- A high-powered window fan
- 4-mil. heavy-duty plastic, translucent enough to let light pass through but not transparent enough to let an image be seen through it. (To test, hold your hand six inches away from the plastic; if you cannot see your hand through the material, then it is opaque enough.) Heavy-duty white drop cloth, often used by painters, works well. Two 9' x 12' cloths plus one 9' x 6' cloth make a bubble of spectacular size.
- Duct or asbestos freezer tape

Procedure

1. Lay the two 9' x 12' cloths out on the floor, one on top of the other, and seal the two long sides plus one short side with tape.

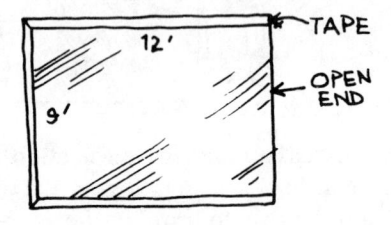

2. Make a 4' x 6' tube out of the 9' x 6' cloth so it can fit around the front of the fan. Tape the long sides of the tube together. Then tape one end of the tube to the untaped end of the bubble and attach the other end to the fan.

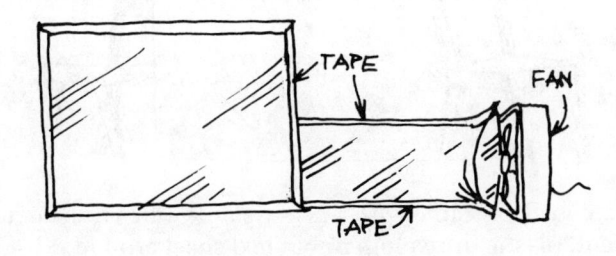

3. Tape the fourth side of the bubble.
4. Turn on the fan. The bubble will inflate in less than three minutes.
5. Now cut in the bubble a 4-foot slit for the door and reinforce it by taping all around the raw edges to keep it from tearing.

A bubble like this will hold at one time 10 to 15 students, depending on their size. Images can be projected onto the outside walls with slide, movie, film loop, overhead or opaque projectors, or any combination of these. The translucent plastic acts as a set of rear-view projection screens for the viewers on the inside. One or several images may be used; the entire surface may be covered with the same image shown on several projectors. With careful coordination, different images may build up to a total bombardment of stimuli that makes a significant impression on children.

Whatever your curriculum, you can project important parts of it onto a media bubble. Here are just a few ideas:

1. To experience the ocean, you can simultaneously project a movie of waves rolling in or splashing against coastal rocks; a set of slides showing life under the sea; the shadow of live goldfish swimming, made by the light of an overhead machine projected through a rectangular glass cake pan filled with water and fish; and a set of diagrams showing wave action—all of this accompanied by appropriate wave sounds, narration or music.

2. If you are studying human physiology, you can project slides of a cross-section of the heart (these may be the same image from two or more projectors) on all of the walls and accompany these with appropriate throbbing sounds; children crawling through the bubble will be able to internalize the miracle of the beating heart.

3. If you're studying the trip on the Mayflower, you can project slides showing the hold of a sailing ship, tipping the projector back and forth at the same time a movie is projecting a raging storm at sea and a tape is sending out roaring wind sounds.

4. Media bubbles make good time capsules. A bubble can become a cave, farm, mine, factory, spaceship, forest, palace, prison, tree house, island, horror chamber or dream home.[8] Children can project their own drawings onto the bubble using opaque or overhead projectors to make the bubble into their own created world.

---

[8]Our special thanks to Priscilla Smith, a fifth grade teacher at Willard School, Evanston, Ill., for many of these ideas.

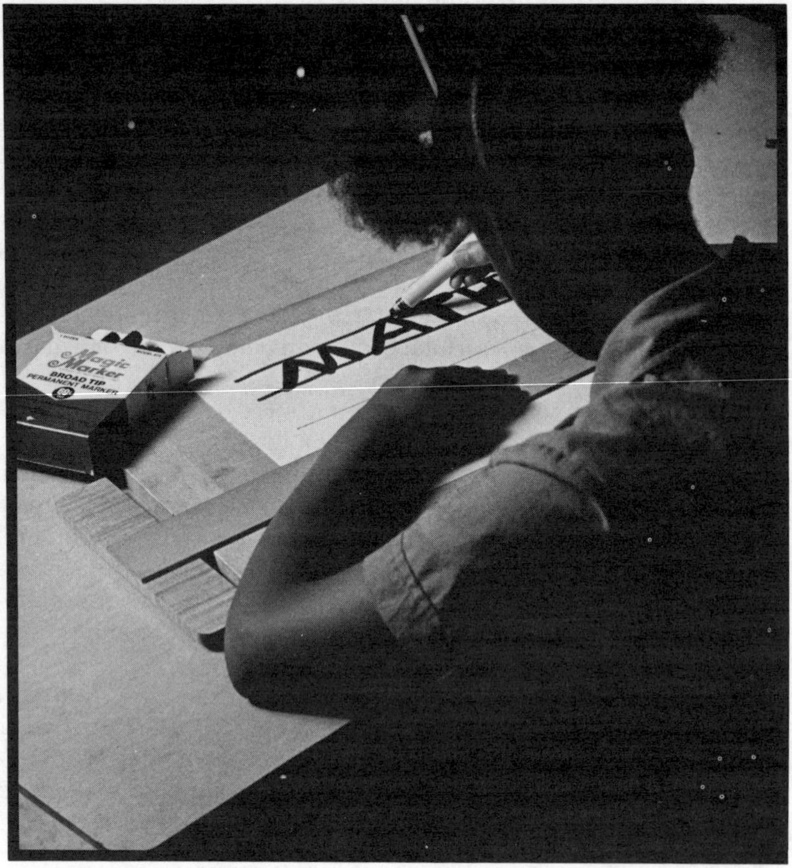
Magic Marker
BROAD TIP
PERMANENT MARKER

4
Lettering

The goal of classroom sign making is to present clear, unambiguous, understandable words. Following are some simple lettering techniques that call for a minimal investment of time or money but will enable you to make effective and readable signs to label such areas as learning stations, classroom museums, bulletin boards or other displays.

QUALITIES OF GOOD LETTERING

Four qualities determine the effectiveness of lettered signs: size of the letters; spacing between the letters, words, numbers or lines: contrast of the letters with the background; and style of lettering.

Appropriate Size
All classroom lettering should be large enough to be read easily from the farthest distance from the sign. This can be assured by following some general guidelines.

Opaque Letters
These appear on flash cards, classroom charts, graphs, collections, bulletin board displays, felt boards and lists of directions at learning stations. To assure readability, follow this guide:

Maximum Distance from the Sign	Minimum Size of Lower Case Letters
8 feet	1/4 inch
16 feet	1/2 inch
32 feet	1 inch
64 feet	2 inches

Projected Letters
These appear on slides, filmstrips, overhead transparencies and films. Just as with opaque lettering, maximum expected viewing distance determines minimum letter size, which is computed by what is generally referred to as the 6W legibility rule. To apply this rule, measure the horizontal width of the material to be projected and then hold that material six times that width away from you. If you can easily read the lettering at this distance, you will, in all probability, be able to read the lettering when it is projected, as long as you are not more than six times the width of the projected image away from the screen or wall on which the image appears.

Good Spacing
When spacing between letters, words or lines is either too little or too much, the written information can be difficult to read; this is because the reader becomes more involved in interpreting the design or configuration of letters than in receiving the intended message. Make sure your spacing affords easy readability.

Optimum Contrast
For lettering purposes, contrast means the relationship of the letters to the background on which they are placed. The goal is to provide enough contrast so that the words are clearly visible from the farthest spot in the room, but not so sharp a distinction that the sign causes eye strain. Although highly contrasting black letters on a pure white background are easy to read from a long distance, they may not be desirable for viewing under very bright room conditions or over a long period. Dark blue letters on a light-blue background or black on a buff or cream-colored surface would be easier on the eyes.

If the background of a sign is multicolored or textured, adequate contrast may be effected by using bolder letters or by shadowing the letters to make them look as if they are standing out from the background.

Unless there is a special reason for a particular background, such as using a photograph as a background for a sign, it is usually better to use cool colors (green, blue, gray) for the background and warm colors (red, orange, purple) for titles. Work for maximum contrast without producing eye strain.

Simple Letter Style
The letter style you choose will influence the legibility of the words or numerals you write. Elaborate or ornate letters are more difficult to read than simple ones such as Sans Serif or Gothic. Unless there is

a special curriculum need to use an ornate print style such as Old English, it is better to stay with less stylized lettering. As with other lettering decisions, your guide should be that any word in the classroom should be easy to read from a point farthest from the sign and under the normally prevailing lighting conditions in the classroom.

LAYOUT

Often, lettering problems can be solved by the use of simple mechanical aids, such as a drawing board, a "T" square and a pair of triangles. These tools are sold at most large stationery or art supply stores, and are relatively inexpensive. Mastering their use is well worth the effort because they'll enable you to improve the quality of the signs you make. With such tools, the task of laying out a full sheet of lettering, properly spaced and aligned, becomes quick and easy.

Recommended Tools and Materials
The starred items are necessary; the others, desirable:
- Drawing board*
  Chipboard or any flat wooden surface, will do.
- "T" square*
- Two triangles*, one 45° x 45° x 90°, and one 30° x 60° x 90°
- Masking tape*
- Soft no. 2 or 2H lead pencils*
- Art gum or pink pearl eraser*
- Paper that both accepts ink well and erases without a smudge—tagboard or high-grade construction paper are preferable*
- Felt markers, speedball pen with a selection of nibs or a Wrico brush pen and India ink[1]*
- Mechanical drawing compass with a lead tip
- Circle template or Pacemaker Protractor
- Graph paper

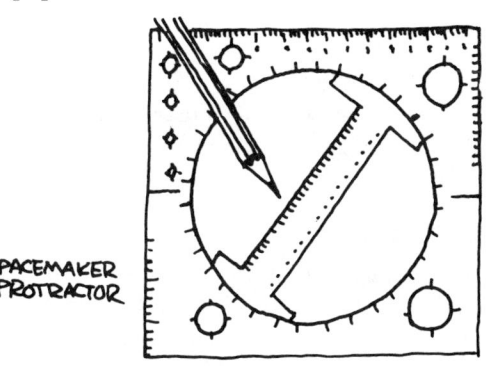

PACEMAKER
PROTRACTOR

[1]See the section on Wrico lettering in this chapter.

45

Procedure
1. Attach the paper to the drawing board with masking tape, making sure it is aligned exactly with the "T" square.
2. Using a soft lead pencil, lightly draw horizontal guidelines, allowing adequate space for each line of lettering and for the space between the lines of words.

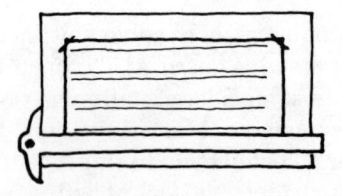

3. Draw light vertical pencil lines to help insure that letters will be consistently vertical.

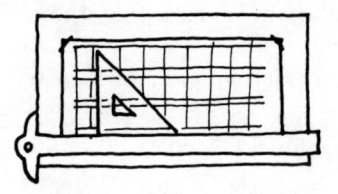

If you prefer slanted letters, use diagonal guidelines, which can be drawn by using the triangles as illustrated in the accompanying drawing.

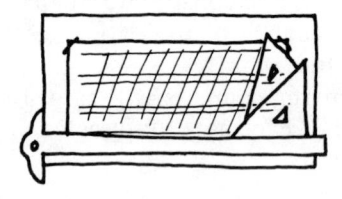

4. Using a soft lead pencil, lightly sketch within the guidelines the letters you desire.
5. Darken the penciled letters with a felt marker, speedball pen and nib with India ink, Wrico brush pen or pencil.
6. Erase the guidelines, leaving only the darkened letters.

LETTERING GUIDES
There are several inexpensive and effective guides for letters, all of which insure uniform results. This does not mean that freehand printing is never recommended. On the contrary, for most classroom signs, especially those that are changed frequently, simple freehand lettering is the fastest and most appropriate way to proceed. If, how-

ever, you would like to expand your range and add other styles to your signs, you may decide to use a lettering guide or gummed letters.

Stencil Lettering
Cardboard or plastic stencil letters, such as the ones that are a part of many standard 12″ rulers, are simple to use and available in a wide variety of lettering styles.

The Unistencil
This simple lettering guide will enable you to construct upper case block letters quickly and easily. It is useful to have a set of them ranging in size from 1″ to 7½″. You can make them for pennies, and once you have the basic template or stencil, duplicating them is easy.

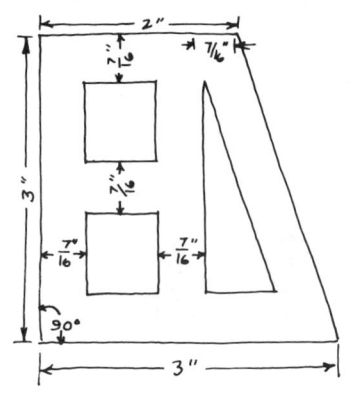

The unistencil may be any size that meets your needs, but the basic proportion of the top to the left side and bottom must remain the same: a 2 to 3 ratio. To make a unistencil you will need the starred drawing tools and materials listed on page 45 plus a steel-edged rule and poster board. See the accompanying illustration to learn how to use the unistencil for block letters.

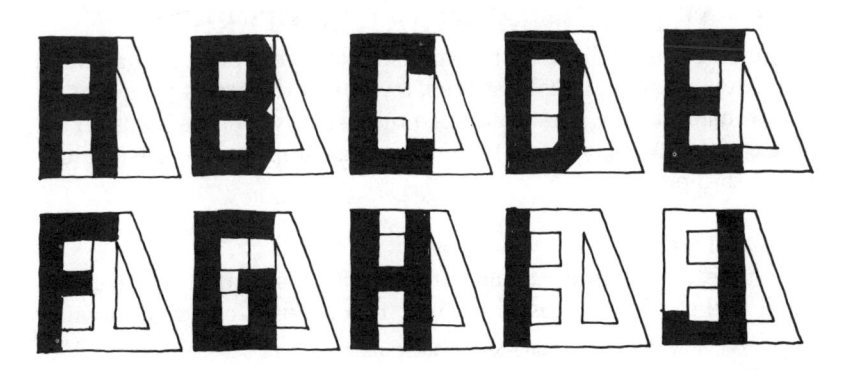

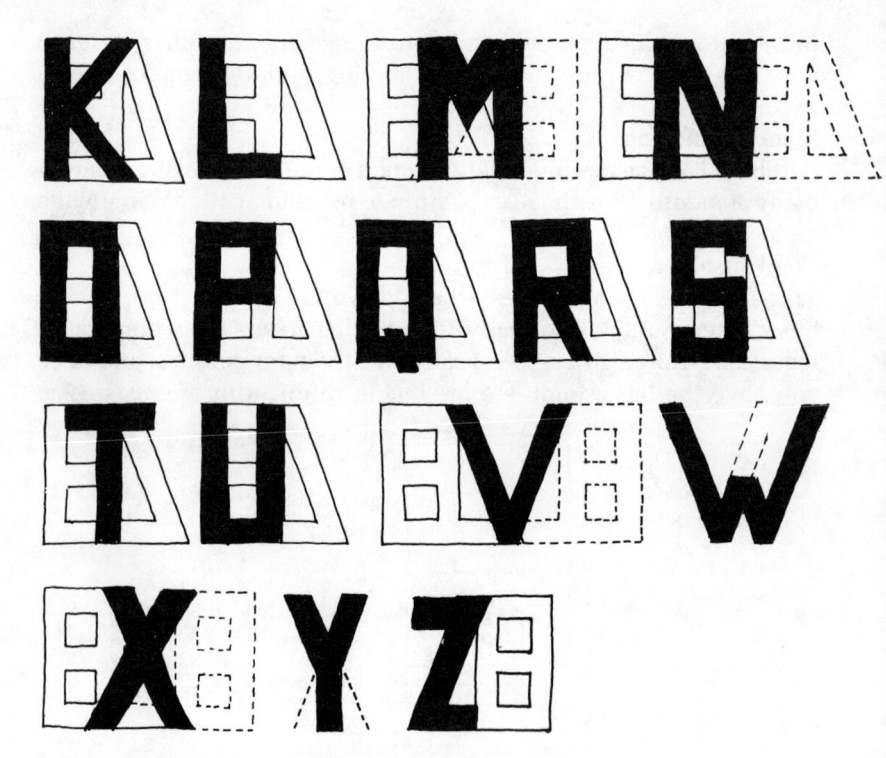

Wrico Lettering
This type of lettering will allow more flexibility with considerable ease, once you have mastered the technique. A Wrico set can be used as a guide for both upper and lower case letters as well as numerals, unlike the unistencil, which can be used only for capital letters. In a Wrico set there are patterns for letters in a variety of sizes from ⅜" to 4". The kit is fairly expensive but will last almost indefinitely.[2]

PREPARED COMMERCIAL LETTERS

If you can afford a little more expensive lettering process than hand lettering or using stencil patterns, try one of the forms of pre-cut or dry transfer letters. The difference in cost may well be justified because of the time saved and the professional appearance and durability of the lettering.

Pre-Cut Letters
Pre-cut letters generally come with gummed backs that can be moistened and stuck on a poster or sign. The Holes-Webway Company[3]

---

[2]Wrico Sign-Maker, The Wood-Regan Instrument Co., 15 Label Street, Montclair, N.J. 07042.

sells the letters in several sizes and colors in boxes with separate compartments for each letter and numeral. A money-saving way to use the pre-cut letters is to trace around them, enabling you to use them over and over so one set can serve many times. Another way to save money is to temporarily mount the letters on bulletin boards using pins or tacks; then the letters themselves can be reused on later signs.

Dry Transfer Letters
These letters provide perhaps the best and most professional looking letters short of a large investment in equipment. They are available in a wide variety of styles and sizes and are often used by commercial artists and printing companies. Your investment is in the cost of the sheet of letters you choose and the time it takes to transfer them. Such companies as Letraset, Artype, Paratype, Chartpak and Normatype sell the letters, which come mounted on a plastic or coated sheet in such a way that when rubbed from the front surface they will transfer and adhere to almost any smooth surface, including paper, cardboard, plastic, glass, metal or painted material. The sheets are all the same size, and the number of letters you get will vary according to the size of the letters you choose.

The simplest way to use these letters is to lay out your sign or poster with light horizontal guidelines indicating the appropriate spacing between lines. Then remove the protective sheet and place the letter sheet over the poster. Since the letter sheet is always transparent, you can see your guidelines through it. Begin transferring letters by rubbing with a pencil or other burnishing tool on the top surface of the sheet. A wax or colored pencil is best because it is hard enough to transfer the letter effectively but soft enough not to fracture or crack the letter during the transferring process. Place the letters side by side following your penciled guideline. To make the lettering even more permanent, first burnish the letters and then lightly spray them with clear plastic spray or artist's fixative.

Whatever process of lettering you choose, your goal is readability. The best lettering transmits the message without unnecessary interference, or what is sometimes called "visual noise."

[3]Holes-Webway Company, 2815 Clearwater Rd., St. Cloud, Minn. 56301.

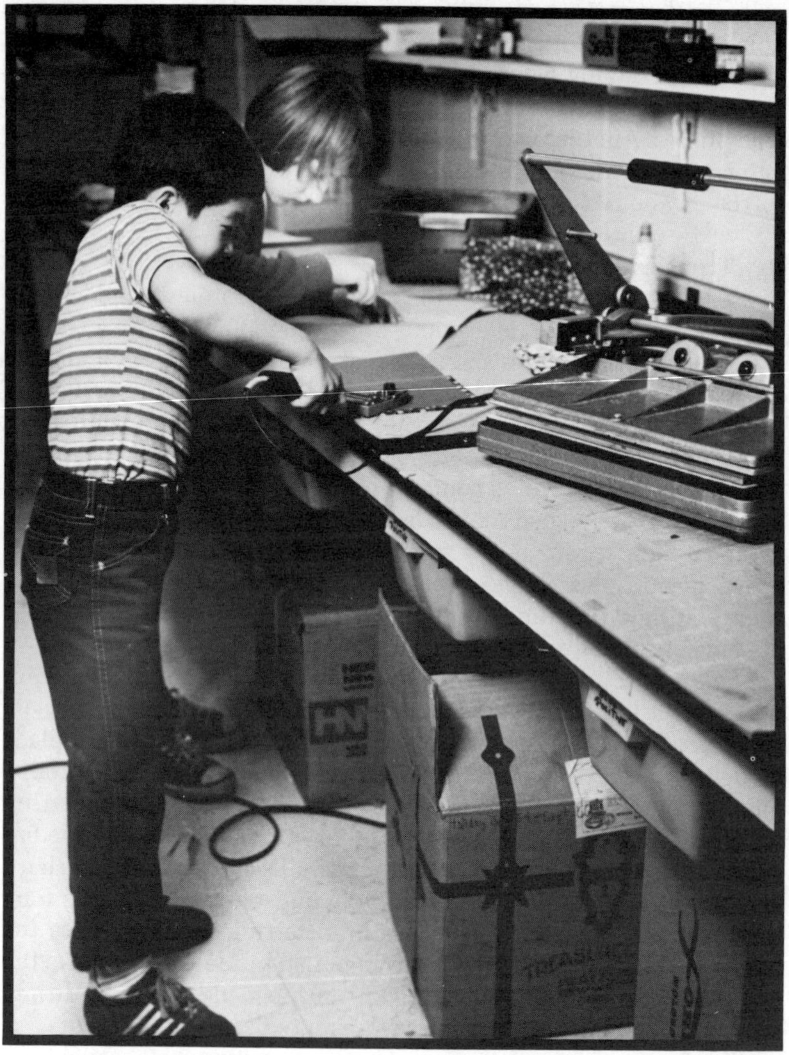

5

Preserving

Written or nonwritten messages, effectively displayed, constitute an important part of a lively learning environment in a classroom. In this chapter we shall describe two processes—mounting and laminating—that will enhance the appeal and permanence of any flat, two-dimensional visual message, be it a chart, map, photograph, picture from a magazine or published work sheet.

RUBBER CEMENT MOUNTING

The materials for this pressure-sensitive process are generally a part of existing school supplies so you may be able to order them using routine requisition procedures. If not, a $10.00 investment at a local art supply or stationery store should be enough for a start.

Recommended Tools and Materials
- Good quality rubber cement (most economically purchased by the gallon)
- Rubber cement thinner, sometimes labeled "Benzol"
- A small container, preferably one with a dispenser brush attached to the lid
  Rubber cement should be stored in a jar or can in a dark place to keep it from hardening. If it does get hard, add thinner and let it set for a couple of days before using it again.
- A steel-edge or flexible steel ruler with nonslip backing
- A cutting tool such as a single-edge razor blade and holder, x-acto knife or scissors
- Railroad board or tagboard that will not take a stain from rubber cement

- Newsprint (blank newspaper stock) or other clean throwaway paper[1]
- Wax paper
- A clean cloth

Procedure for a Temporary Mounting

1. Select the visual to be mounted and trim it to the exact shape and size you wish to show.

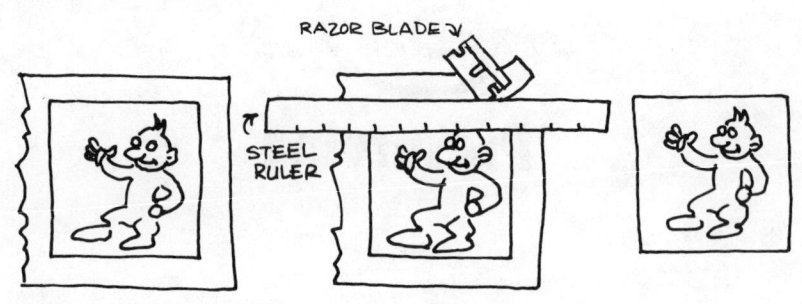

2. Select or trim railroad board or tagboard somewhat larger than the visual. Use a color that will highlight or complement the visual.

3. Place the visual on the backing board so an equal space extends beyond it on two sides and at the top and a larger space appears at the bottom (this allows room for a title). Measure with a ruler and make light pencil marks on the backing to indicate where each corner of the visual is to be placed.

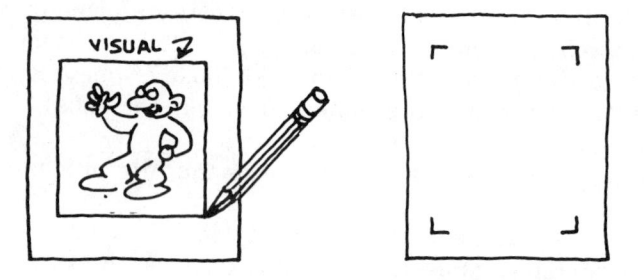

4. Remove the visual and place it face down on the newsprint; put your backing board face up next to it.

5. Apply an even coat of rubber cement (as it comes from the jar) on the back of the visual. Be sure to apply the glue from the center of the picture out toward the edge, making sure no cement gets under the picture where it may loosen the ink.

[1]Your local newspaper office may be a source of free newsprint. Often the ends of large rolls are given away.

The newsprint will catch the extra rubber cement.

6. While the rubber cement is still wet, quickly reposition the visual onto the backing board using your light pencil marks as your guide. Using a pencil or a pen, press against the visual to squeeze out any excess cement, and then allow the mounted picture to dry. Once again, be careful not to get any rubber cement on the front surface of the visual. If there are wrinkles, smooth them out.

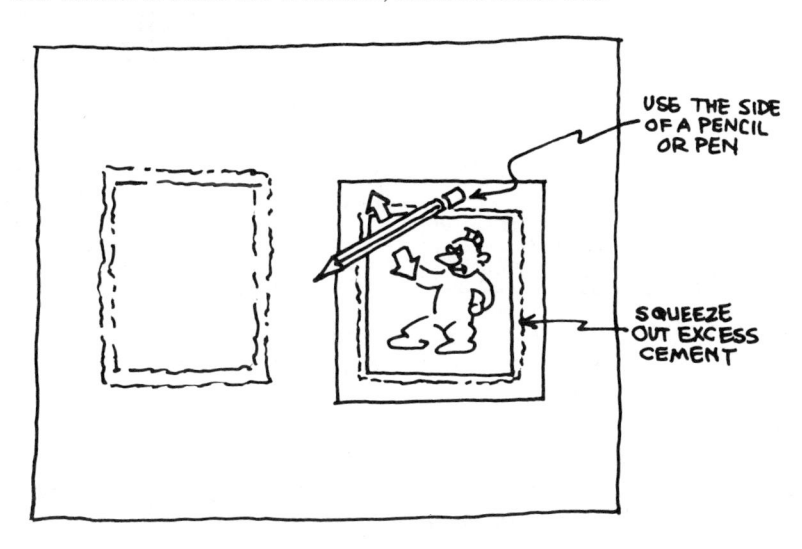

7. When the cement has dried, take a clean cloth and rub off any excess that has appeared at the edges of the visual. This will rub off easily and should not damage the picture. Gently rub down the entire visual to be sure you have a good bond.

8. Examine the completed work and erase any visible pencil marks. Your temporary rubber cement mounting is now ready to display.

Procedure for a Permanent Mounting

This process effects a more permanent rubber cement mounting.

1. Add rubber cement thinner to rubber cement in the following proportion:

    1/3 cement thinner

    2/3 rubber cement

Now stir the contents to an even consistency.

2. Repeat steps 1 to 4 for a temporary mounting.

3. Put rubber cement on the back of the visual and on the front of the backing board. To insure good coverage, apply the cement beyond the pencil marks placed on your backing card. Let this dry.

4. Cover the backing board with wax paper, leaving only about ¼" of the area above the pencil marks that has cement on it exposed at the top; this will allow initial positioning of the visual.

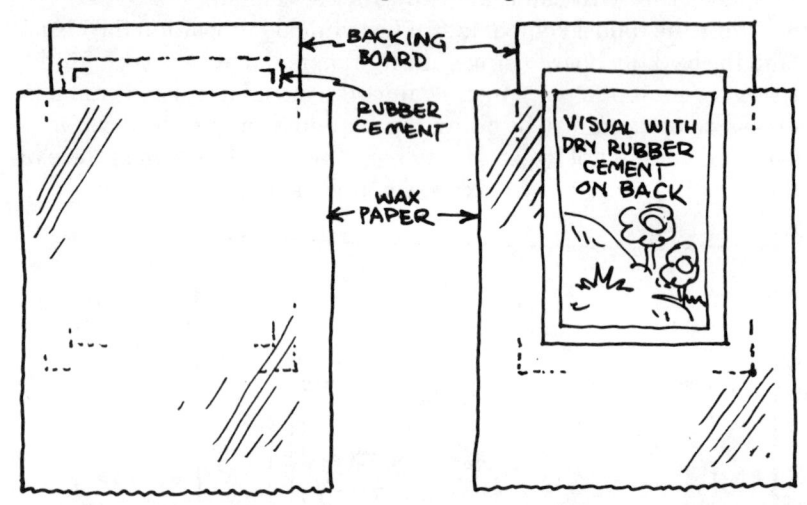

5. Now place the visual on top of the wax paper and position it with the guide marks. Press the top lightly against the cement on the backing board; slowly remove the wax paper and continue to apply pressure to the visual from the top to the bottom. Keep in mind that once the two cemented surfaces come into contact, they adhere permanently in a suction-type bond. Try not to trap any bubbles of air between the two surfaces because they will be difficult to remove.

6. Rubbing gently with a clean cloth, remove any excess rubber cement that may be exposed around the edges of the mounted visual.
7. Examine the work and remove any pencil marks that may still be showing. You now have a permanently mounted visual. If you are planning to mount a number of visuals, you may find it convenient to pre-glue several backing boards at once a few hours or days before you actually use them. The boards will stack and store well providing you do not apply excessive pressure or allow two cemented surfaces to come in contact with each other.

HOT PRESS MOUNTING

Although rubber cement mounting is effective, it is not necessarily the most efficient or best way to mount flat materials. Hot press, or dry mounting, is a heat-sensitive process that gives essentially the same results as rubber cement mounting, but in less time and with a far more permanent effect. Once you understand the principle of the hot press and the number of adhesives available, you probably will find hot press mounting superior to other techniques. Most children above third grade can safely work with the equipment, enabling them to dry mount two-dimensional materials.

You may use an ordinary household iron at settings from the lowest to the middle of the synthetic fabric settings for all of the processes described here. However, you will probably find it simpler to use a basic hot press, which is already a part of the equipment of many school systems. Although the initial investment for it may seem high, this type of equipment will last a long time with little or no maintenance. It is not uncommon to have a press last 15 to 20 years under very heavy usage.

Recommended Equipment and Materials

The starred items are necessary, the others desirable:
- Hot press or home iron set at cotton setting*
- Tacking iron or tip of home iron*

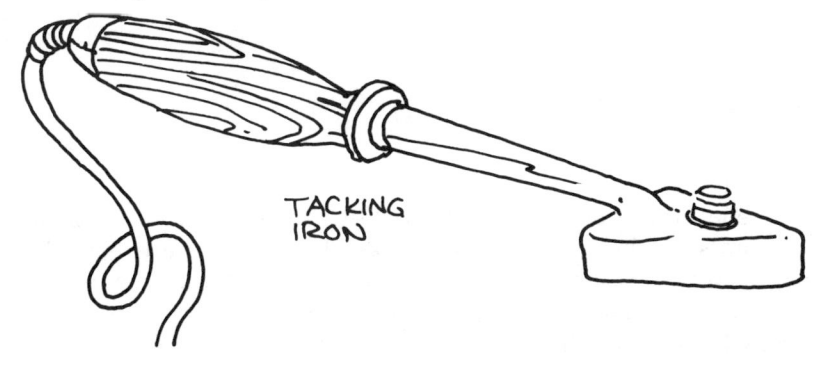

- Dry mounting tissue*
- Railroad or similar mounting card stock, such as uncoated gray chipboard*
- Razor blade and holder , x-acto knife or scissors*
- Newsprint (blank newspaper stock) or Kraft paper*
- Steel-edge or flexible steel ruler*
- Other materials to use with hot press, such as Fotoflat (temporary tissue), Chartex (cloth backing material) and laminating film (Mylar film)
- Chipboard or other cutting surface

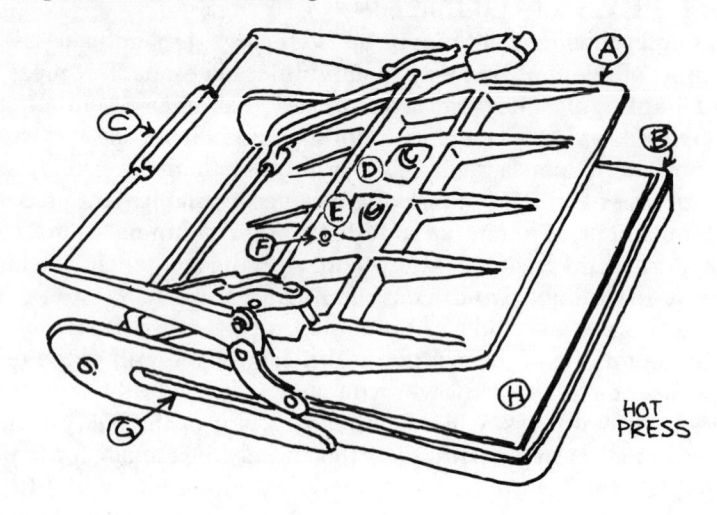

HOT PRESS

A The heating element

B A rubber pad with a felt cover

C The handle used to close the press and apply the required pressure

D Thermostat control (180°F. to 350°F.)

E Green light to indicate that the desired heat level has been reached

F On and off switch

G Cantilever design to allow for large card dry mounting

H Press board

Procedure
1. Preheat the household iron to slightly above the warm setting or the press to the machine's recommended temperature (usually around 225° F.). Close but do not lock the press for preheating.
2. Select a visual, but do not trim it; a rough cut picture (or snapshot with a border on it) is easier to use than a trimmed one.

3. Select a blank sheet of newsprint and place the picture face down on this clean surface.

4. Select the appropriate size of mounting tissue (slightly larger than the picture) and tack this to the back of the picture, which is still face down on the newsprint, by pressing it lightly with a tacking iron in the center of the tissue. If you leave the tacking iron on the dry mounting tissue for just a few seconds, the glue will not stick to the iron.

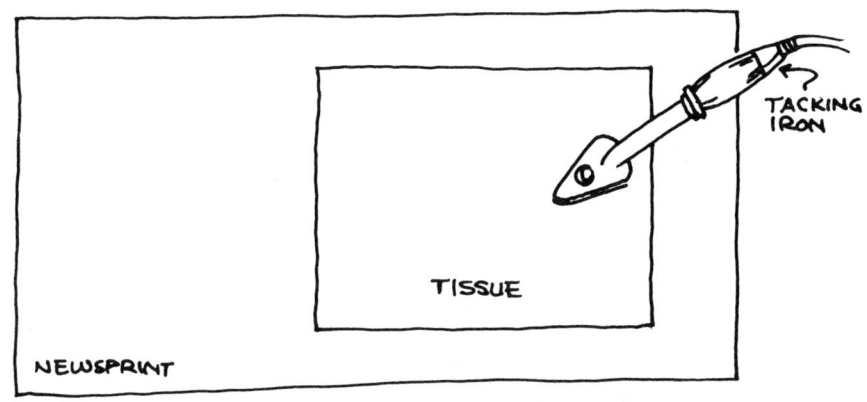

5. Now take the picture with the tissue tacked in place off the newsprint and place it face up on the cutting board.

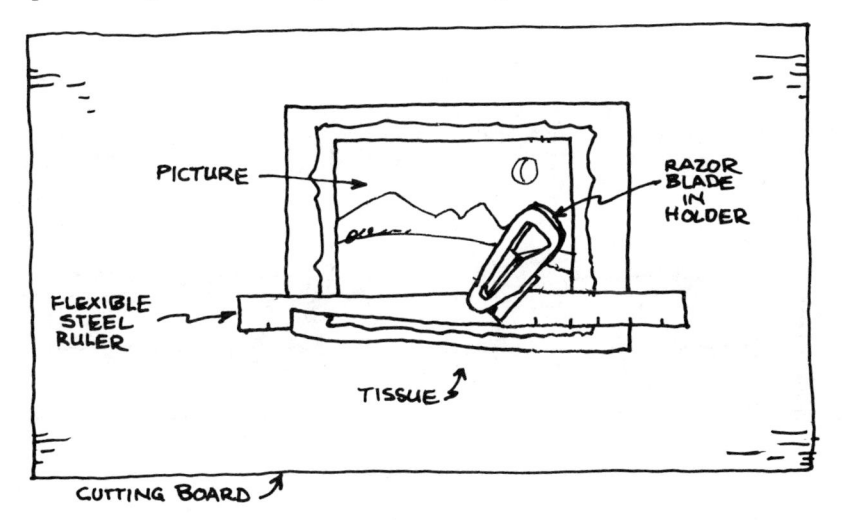

6. Trim the picture using a razor blade and flexible steel ruler, being sure to cut both the picture and the tissue at the same time. (Scissors or other cutting tools can be used, but they are not as efficient.)

57

7. Now that the picture has been trimmed, select an appropriate mounting board and position it under the visual as desired. (We recommend that the board extend beyond the picture equally on the top and both sides, and that it extend a bit more beyond the bottom.)

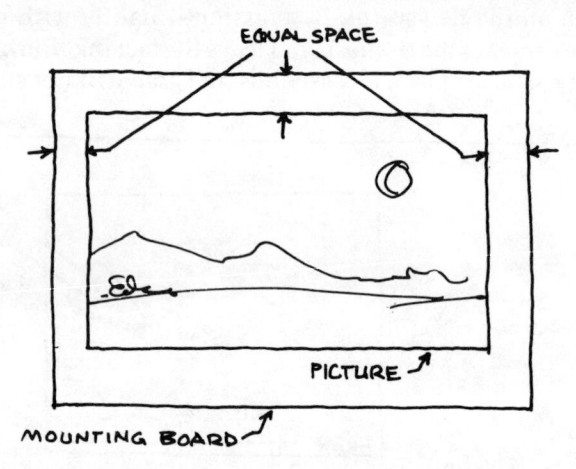

8. Tack only the tissue, not the picture and the tissue, to the mounting board in two diagonally opposite corners. If you tack the tissue to the four corners now, you will be more likely to get bubbles.

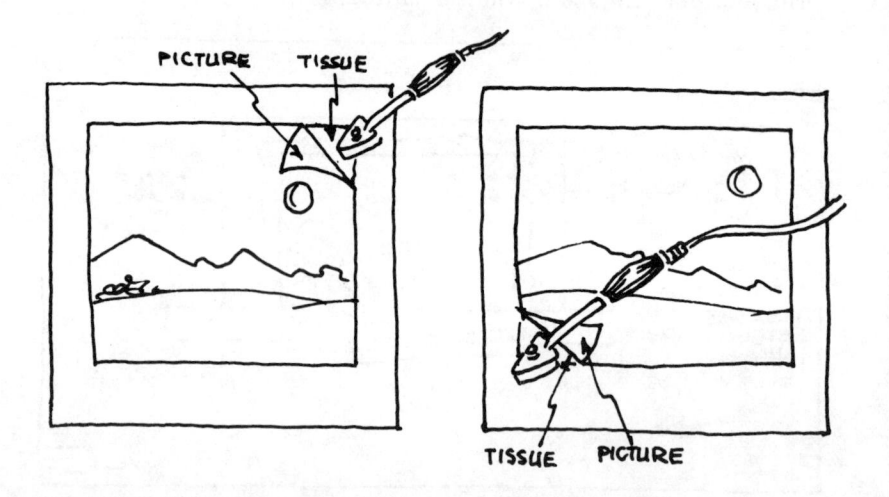

9. Put the picture, dry mounting tissue and mounting board on one side of the newsprint and fold over the other side of the newsprint to completely enclose the graphic.

10. Open the hot press, insert the covered visual, close and lock the

press and heat for 5 to 40 seconds (the desired time will depend on the thickness of your visual). If you're using a household iron, iron the encased visual at slightly above the warm setting.

11. Remove the mounted visual from the press, take it out of the newsprint and inspect it for good adhesion. Should there be any bubbles under the picture, repeat steps 8 and 9 and heat again. This usually solves the problem. Your visual is now ready for use.

Other Mounting Materials
Hot press mounting can be done with other materials:
1. *Fotoflat* is a dry mounting tissue that is thicker and effects a less permanent bond than regular dry mounting tissue. However, it has four advantages: it adheres well to textured surfaces such as wool felt backing for felt board manipulatives[2]; it effects a removable adhesion, which can be unbonded by reheating[3]; it is better for mounting thin visuals because it is white, not amber like most dry mounting tissue; and it makes possible the mounting of some photographs that are subject to damage by high temperatures. Fotoflat also is a good adhesive for book binding, especially when the cover material is heavy, and for preserving delicate items. When using Fotoflat, preheat the hot press at 180° F. rather than 225° and leave the mounting in for one minute. A household iron should be set at the lowest end of the dial.
2. *Chartex* is a cloth backing material with adhesive on only one side. This mounting material, which usually comes in a roll 36" x 25', is useful for reinforcing thin paper or helping preserve things like maps and charts that tend to get rough handling. Classroom materials that are mounted with Chartex and then laminated (see the following section) will have a longer than normal life.

The process for mounting with Chartex is the same as for mounting with dry mounting tissue; keep the temperature of the hot press at 225° F. and leave the mounting in the press for only five seconds. A household iron should be set at slightly above the warm setting. (High temperatures or extended periods in the press may cause the adhesive to penetrate the cloth.) Chartex is not intended to be used for mounting to a cardboard backing; the Chartex itself becomes the backing.

[2]See Chapter 2 for more on felt board projects.
[3]To remove Fotoflat-mounted material, wrap it in newsprint, place it in the press and close the plate so it rests on the material; do not lock the press. Reapply heat at 220° F. for about 60 seconds. Immediately lift the press, remove the material and slowly peel the material from the Fotoflat, starting in one corner. If any of the adhesive remains, remove it with a little cleaning fluid.

LAMINATING

Laminating is as easy as the mounting processes just described and can sometimes be performed at the same time. Essentially it is a preserving process, whereby a paper surface is coated with a thin layer of plastic, protecting it from wear and providing other advantages as well. For example, laminated paper or laminated mounted visuals can be drawn or written on with crayon or water-soluble felt markers and later erased; they also can be written on with a permanent ink for long-term use. Laminating preserves inexpensive paper such as newsprint from the yellowing effects of oxidation, thereby prolonging its life. Certain pictures can be transformed into materials for projecting, such as overhead transparencies or 2" x 2" slides.[4]

Contact Paper Process

If a hot press is not available or if your children are too young or inexperienced to work safely with one, you can laminate with ordinary transparent adhesive shelf paper, sometimes called Contact paper. It is commonly sold in dime and hardware stores and in the housewares sections of department stores. Contact paper has an adhesive already attached to it that is covered by protective paper. To use it, you need only a scissors or a razor blade, a ruler, a cutting board and an ordinary kitchen spoon.

1. Select a mounted or unmounted picture to be laminated. Decide if you want the visual to be protected on one or both sides.
2. Lay the visual on a clean flat surface; a smooth laminated plastic desk top is ideal.
3. Cut the clear shelf paper slightly larger than the visual, making sure not to remove the protective backing.

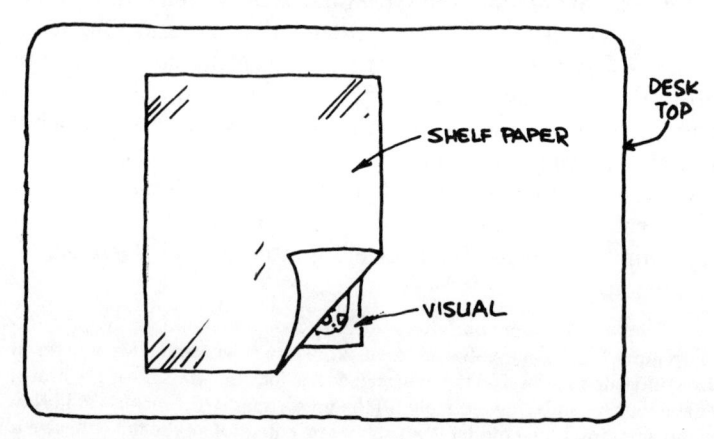

[4]See "Color Lifting" in Chapter 8.

4. Start the laminating process by removing a small portion of the protective backing from the shelf paper and sticking it partly to the flat surface and partly to the visual.

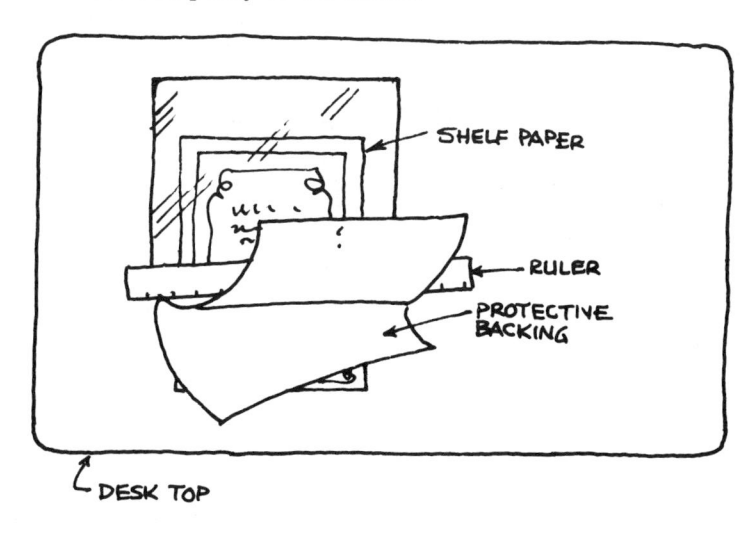

5. Draw a ruler firmly down and across the entire surface to be laminated, simultaneously removing the protective backing, until the visual is totally covered with the protective plastic material. For better adhesion, rub the surface with a metal spoon or the back of a plastic comb.
6. Remove the entire visual from the desk top or other flat surface and examine it closely for bubbles or grayish areas. Repeat the rubbing if any are found. If you wish to laminate both sides, turn the visual over and repeat all the steps.
7. Place the laminated visual on a cutting board and trim it to the finished size. You now have a completely protected visual.

Hot Press Process
A hot press can be used to laminate any flat material that is not adversely affected by heat or that does not have a highly polished or plastic surface.
Recommended Materials
- Laminating film
- Scissors, razor blade and holder or x-acto knife
- Tacking iron or electric household iron
- Newsprint (black newspaper stock)
- Steel-edge or flexible steel ruler
- Pressboard or piece of ¼" masonite (optional)

Procedure for an Unmounted Visual
1. Select the visual to be mounted (leave it untrimmed) and preheat the hot press to 270° F.
2. Cut a piece of laminating film that is twice the size of the visual, allowing at least ¼" margin of film all around.

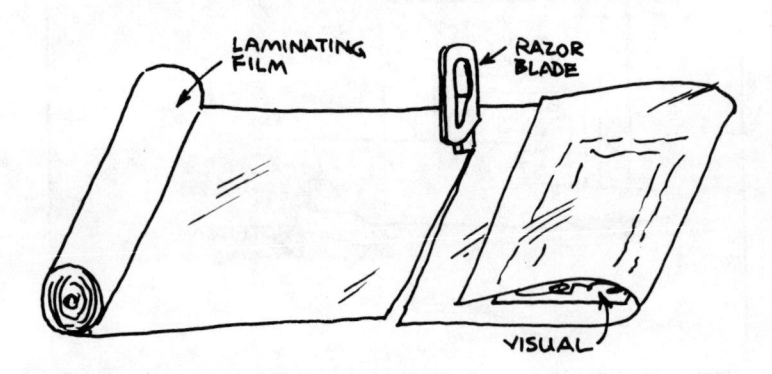

3. Enclose the visual within the laminating film, placing the dull side next to the visual and the polished side out.
4. With a tacking iron, tack the laminating film in about three or four places around the edge of the visual, being careful not to touch what will be a part of the finished surface. These tacks will hold the visual in place while it is being moved to the press.

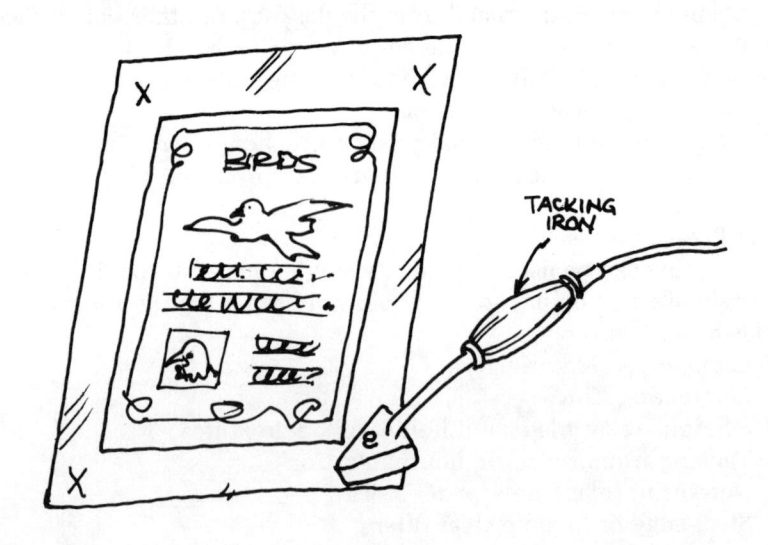

5. Put the plastic-covered visual within a folded piece of newsprint to fully protect its surfaces, and then place it in the hot press. Close and lock the press, letting it heat for about 60 seconds. (If additional pressure is needed, you can place a ¼" piece of masonite or pressboard beneath the heating visual.) When you remove the visual, inspect it to see if it has been completely laminated. If not, reheat it again for another 60 seconds. If you are laminating something small, such as an I.D. card, you can use an iron set at the middle of the synthetic fabric setting, but don't attempt to laminate something larger without a hot press.

6. Trim the excess laminating film from the picture with a razor blade and ruler or with a paper cutter or scissors.

Procedure for a Mounted Visual

To laminate a mounted visual, follow the mounting process described on pages 51–59 and the laminating process just presented.

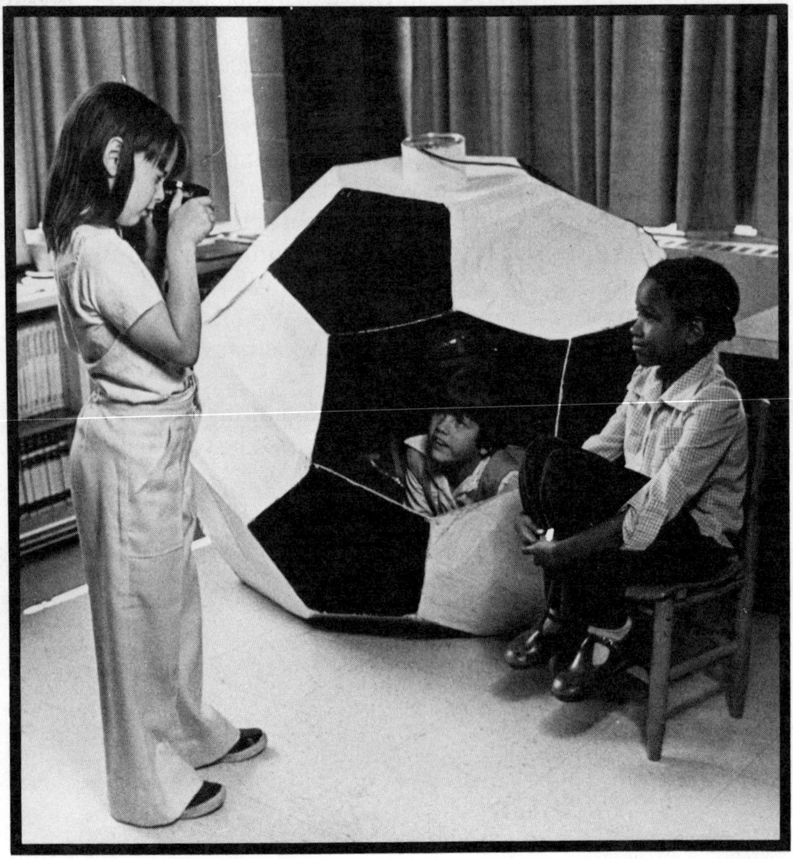

6
Photographing

The popular hobby of photography can enhance classroom learning in many ways. For example, children can make their own 2" x 2" slides or black and white or color prints to illustrate their stories, promote new composition or focus on detail in science study; they also can bring historical material to life by setting up and then photographing scenes from the past.

Still photography using an inexpensive camera and black and white film is well worth the investment. Even without a camera, however, students can experiment with photographic processes and can develop pictures.

PHOTOGRAM
This project will acquaint you with the basic principles of photography: exposing a light-sensitive paper to light and then putting the exposed paper into appropriate chemical solutions to develop and fix an image. The mystery and thrill of seeing the photographic paper come alive with an image is unforgettable for the novice. Older students often get interested in studying the chemical changes and scientific principles involved in the phototechnology.

Setting Up a Darkroom
A Closet, Washroom or Storage Alcove
Be sure you have an incandescent light fixture or a 110–120 volt outlet in the room. In addition you will need:
- A safelight bulb, which can be bought at a camera store
- Another light source with a floodlight bulb
  A hanging flashlight will do. Be sure the floodlight is separated

from the safelight so students won't mistake one for the other.
- Three flat pans large enough to accommodate 8" x 10" paper Plastic developing trays can be bought from a photographic supplier. Your school's science lab or kitchen may have pyrex cake pans that will serve.
- A table big enough for the three pans and an adjacent working area
- A pair of tweezers or spring-type clothespin
- Kodak's Tri-chem Pack, available inexpensively from a photographic supplier

A Portable Darkroom
A large refrigerator or appliance carton can become a portable darkroom by painting it on the inside using a flat black paint (black latex is ideal). If your local hardware store does not have flat black paint, try a theater supply house. Put a table or desk in the box that will hold the developing trays. Then seal up all the openings with black cloth tape, such as Mystik tape. Cut a door at the bottom of the box large enough to walk through and cover it from the inside with a piece of heavy black fabric; make sure the fabric is opaque so light cannot project through it. Heavy flannel, velveteen, old theater drapes, oilcloth or a fabric-backed plastic tablecloth in a dark color will work well. The fabric cover can be taped along the inside top edge of the box with cloth tape.

An extension cord with a fixture for a bulb should now be poked through a hole in the top of the carton. The opening around the cord will need to be very tightly taped to keep light out—black electrical tape is best. A second light source, such as a hanging flashlight, should also be placed inside the box.

Recommended Materials and Equipment for a Photogram
- A permanent or portable darkroom equipped as just described
- A package of 8" x 10" photographic paper, available at a photographic supply store
- A light source, such as a flashlight or spotlight
- An array of opaque, translucent or patterned materials to create various effects on the photographic paper
  Try simple, everyday materials such as nylon hose, lace eyelet fabric, paper clips, scissors, sea shells, light bulbs, rulers, pencils, paper doilies, dried flowers or leaves or yarn.
- Newsprint or Kraft paper
- A place to allow prints to dry (this does not need to be in a darkroom)
- A watch or clock

The range of subjects for a photogram is restricted only by the imagination: The juxtaposition of any number of familiar objects to create new patterns or images can be thought provoking and pleasing. Once the process is mastered, you may decide to call in a creative arts consultant or local photographer to help you discover new ways to make photograms.

Procedure
1. Arrange a signal so that others will know when the darkroom is in use; this will prevent having the door accidentally opened and overexposing work in progress.
2. In the darkroom, arrange three trays for chemicals on the table, leaving a space for objects and for exposing the film under a light source.
3. Mix the chemicals according to the directions on Kodak's Trichem Pack and put them in the appropriate trays.
4. Check the darkroom to be sure there is no light leakage and that the safelight bulb works. Also be sure the exposing light is bright enough to evenly light all of an 8" x 10" piece of photographic paper when placed under it.
5. Before starting the darkroom process, decide on the objects to be printed and their arrangement. In the darkroom, with only the safelight on, open a package of photographic paper and remove one sheet. Immediately reclose the photographic paper packet. Now put the single sheet of paper face up directly under the exposing light source. Then arrange the objects on the paper and turn on the spotlight or flashlight and expose the photographic paper for 15 to 20 seconds. You will need to experiment to determine the optimum exposure time for your particular light source.
6. Remove the objects and submerge the exposed photographic paper in the tray with the developer solution for approximately 1½ minutes, slowly and gently agitating the tray. The background will turn black and the image will appear.
7. Now place the photographic paper in the stop solution in the second tray for about 15 seconds, agitating the tray continuously.
8. Place the photogram in the final fixer solution, agitating it briefly, and leave it there for five minutes.
9. The process is completed outside the darkroom by first rinsing the photogram under running water for about 20 minutes and then letting it dry on newsprint or Kraft paper, covered with paper towels, for several hours. To speed up the drying, you can put the prints inside a folded sheet of newsprint and then in a hot press[1] at a very low temperature. This will not only dry the print but flatten it as well.

[1]See Chapter 5 for more on hot presses.

STILL PHOTOGRAPH CAMERAS
Self-Made Cartridge Pinhole Camera
Making your own camera is another step in learning basic photographic principles. A cartridge pinhole camera is simply a light-tight box that has the capability of letting an image enter it and exposing the light-sensitive film inside it. Although it costs only pennies, it has the basic elements of any camera: a box, a shutter and film. Since the development of the Instamatic cartridge film, making and using your own camera is easy. Once constructed, this simple box camera is merely transferred from one cartridge to another when all the film is exposed. You take the used film to a processor for developing or develop it yourself. Black and white film is the most appropriate for beginners because it is the least expensive.

Recommended Materials
- A cartridge for 126 black and white film
- A piece of flat card stock about the thickness of a laundry shirt cardboard, 2 ¾" x 11"
- A piece of heavy aluminum foil about 1½" square
- A coin the size of a nickel or penny
- Two strong rubber bands
- A sewing needle
- A small roll of black cloth or masking tape, ¾" or 1" wide
- A black felt-tip marker
- An x-acto knife or a pair of scissors

Procedure

1. Measure and mark the large piece of cardboard this way:

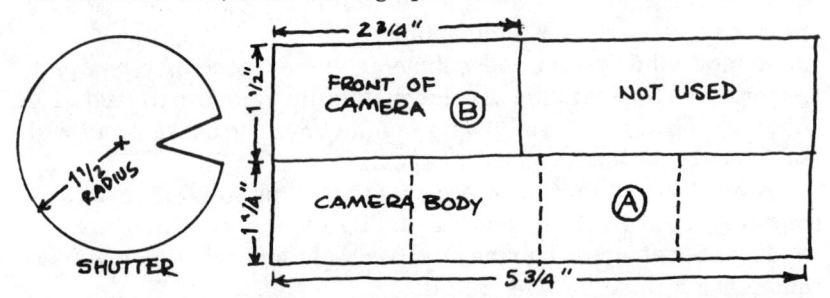

2. Using a razor blade, paper cutter, scissors or x-acto knife, cut the cardboard to separate the 1½" x 2¾" piece for the front of the box camera, the shutter and the larger piece, 1¼" x 5¾". Try to keep all pieces as square and accurate as possible.

3. With an x-acto knife, score the large cardboard piece at 1 7/16" intervals approximately halfway through the cardboard to aid in folding the main camera box.

MAIN CAMERA BODY

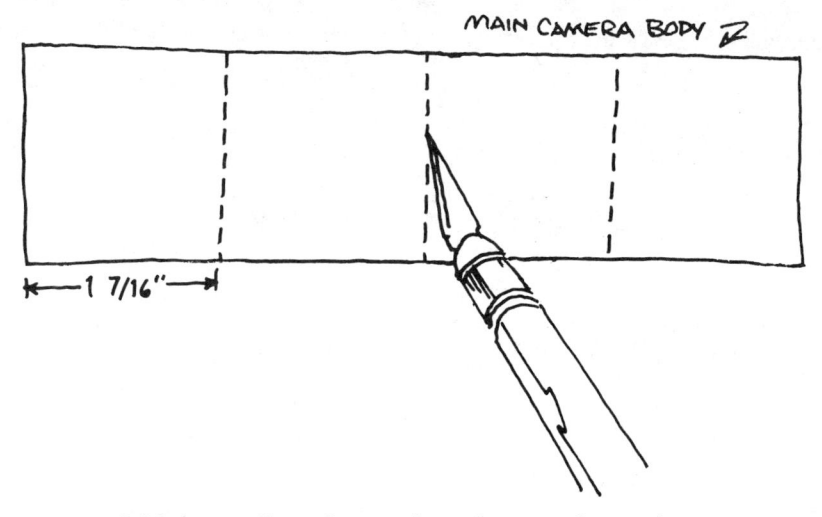

|←—1 7/16"—→|

4. Now fold the cardboard into a box shape and tape the one seam where the ends meet, making sure it is secure and will not leak light.

5. Cut the remaining piece.

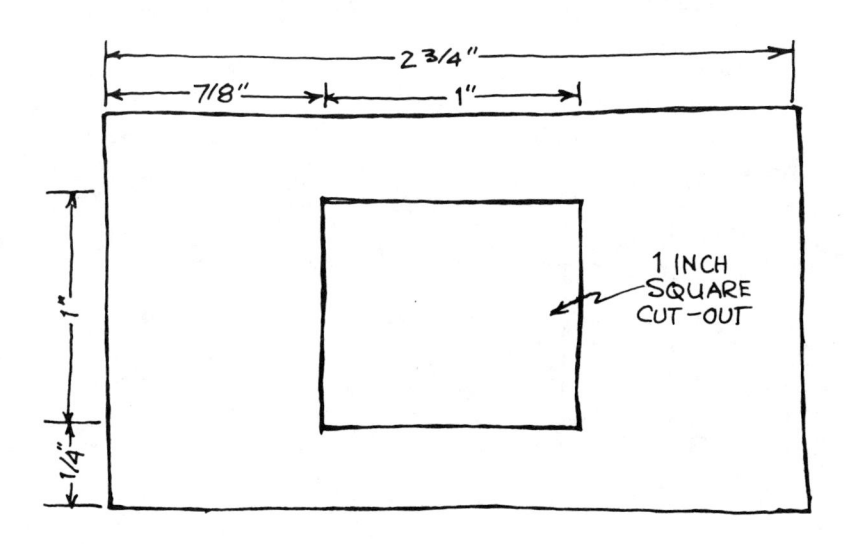

1 INCH
SQUARE
CUT-OUT

6. Tape the piece of aluminum foil over the back of the shutter assembly centering it over the 1" square cutout. Tape it down securely on all four sides.

69

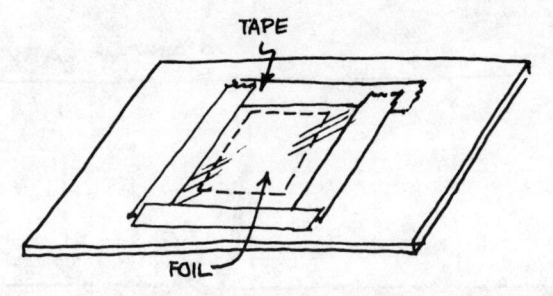

7. Rest the foil on a hard, flat surface. Then draw light diagonal lines to locate the exact center of the shutter opening as shown in this diagram. Puncture a small pinhole with the sewing needle.

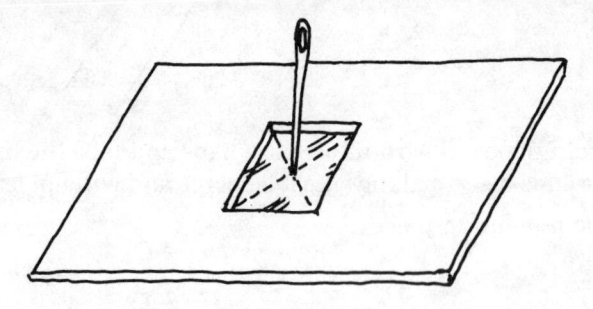

8. Attach the disk, which will act as a shutter, to the front of the camera with a brass paper fastener. It must lie flat against the camera to prevent unwanted light from entering the box, and it must rotate freely.

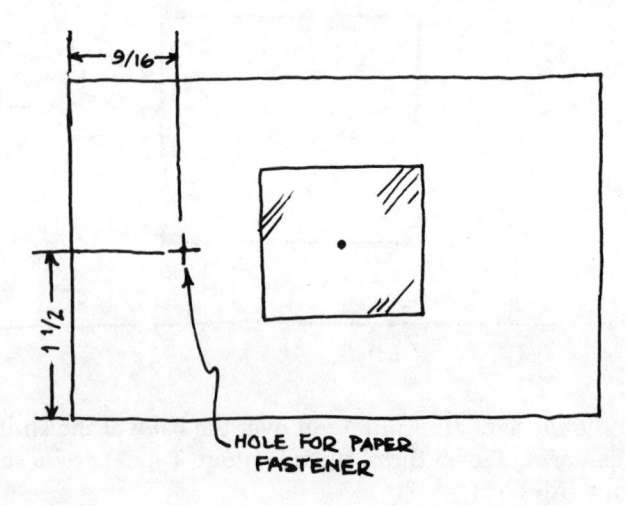

BRASS FASTENER FOR PIVOT POINT

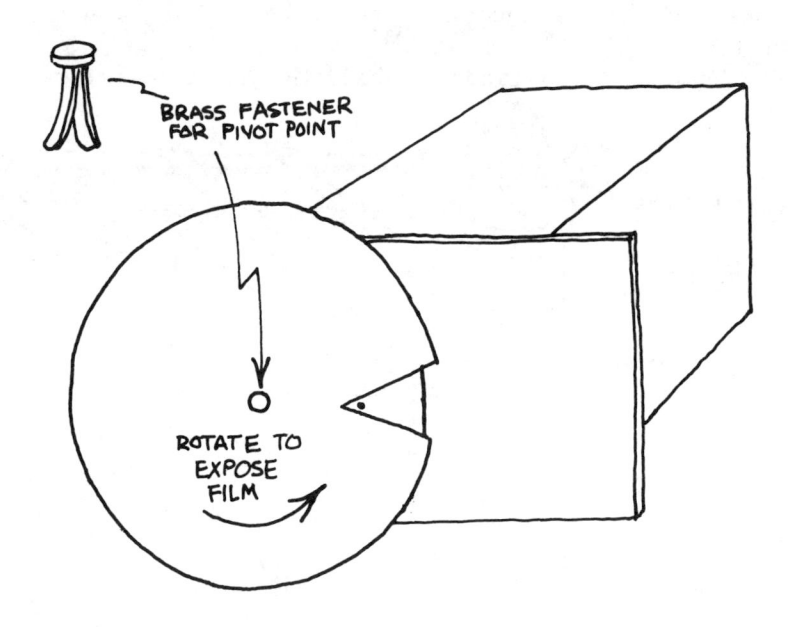

ROTATE TO EXPOSE FILM

9. Tape the shutter assembly over one of the open ends of the box, making sure to center it over the box and to keep the box as square as possible. Use enough tape to insure a secure bond and to prevent any light from entering the box. When the camera is completely assembled and taped, darken any areas inside the box not covered by black masking tape with a black felt-tip marker to prevent light reflection inside the box.

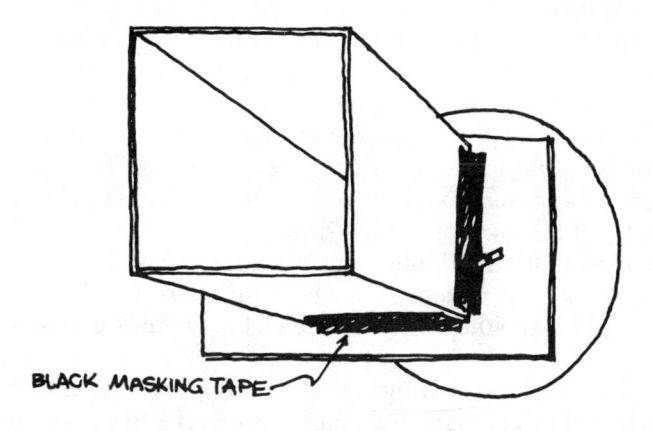

BLACK MASKING TAPE

10. The camera is now ready to attach to the Instamatic cartridge with the two rubber bands. Be sure this is a tight fit to insure no light

leakage and that the shutter is securely in place before you advance the film.

11. You are now ready to advance the film by using a coin in the film

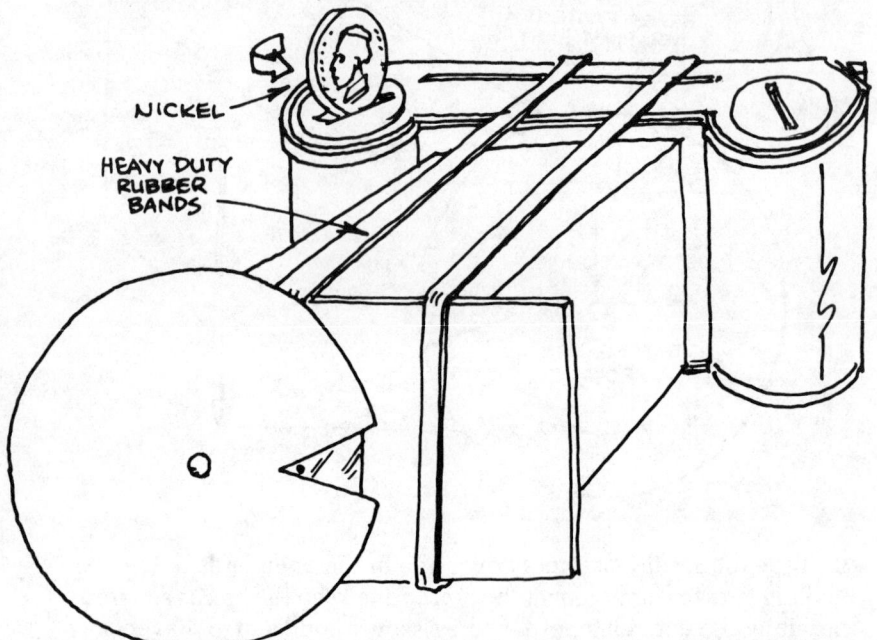

carrier to rotate it counterclockwise. The little opening on the back of the cartridge will show a number on the yellow paper for each picture. Rotate the carrier until the third or fourth duplicate number appears in the opening.

Guidelines for Using

Your camera is now ready for action. Three critical elements of a regular camera are missing in a pinhole camera: a shutter with changeable speeds, a lens for sharp, crisp focus and a viewfinder to determine the exact picture. Although these limitations will not prohibit you from getting a picture, they will limit the quality of your photographs and the flexibility of the camera. You will get the best results if you follow these guidelines:

- Photograph only motionless objects as your first subjects.
- Be sure your camera doesn't move when you expose the film. You may want to tape the camera to a table top or fence post to keep it still.
- Expose your film according to the following chart, which matches the exposure time to the light and speed of the film, as indicated by an ASA number on the box of film. If you cannot find it, ask your photo supply dealer to tell you what it is.

Film Speed ASA Number	Bright Sun	Cloudy Bright
400	1½ to 1 second	2 to 4 seconds
125	2 seconds	8 seconds
80	3 seconds	12 to 15 seconds

- Always take two or three pictures of the same scene, varying the exposure time, and keep a record of how long you exposed each. Then you can compare your best photograph with the exposure time you used and decide which is optimum.

When all the film has been exposed, wind the film tail into the cartridge and take off the camera box. Take the film to a developer or develop it yourself into black and white glossy prints.

Inexpensive Cameras

The Snapshooter,[2] a simple camera to operate, attaches to a film cartridge much as the self-made cartridge pinhole camera does. In addition to the components of the pinhole camera, this camera has a lens, shutter and simple viewfinder that add considerably to the qualtiy and accuracy of photographs. Commercial plastic cameras are, of course, more durable than cardboard ones.

If you can afford a $15.00 to $25.00 camera, however, you will have the advantage of a good fixed focus lens and shutter system; a device that automatically establishes the appropriate amount of light to enter the camera (a photoelectric cell that adjusts the aperture to the amount of light that strikes the film); a film advance mechanism; a simple viewfinder to help you determine the area and subject of the photograph; the capability of shooting indoors or at night, using flash bulbs; and the option of adding a close-up lens.

Even so, the Instamatic camera, like the pinhole and the Snapshooter, has limitations in its adjustment to available light, the movement of the subject and the allowable distance from the camera to the subject. However, if you operate within these limitations, you can take good pictures. Watch for seasonal sales on new cameras or for opportunities to buy used cameras that others have traded in on more expensive types.

[2]Snapshooter cameras can be ordered from Visual Motivations Co., Regal Road, King of Prussia, Pa. 19406.

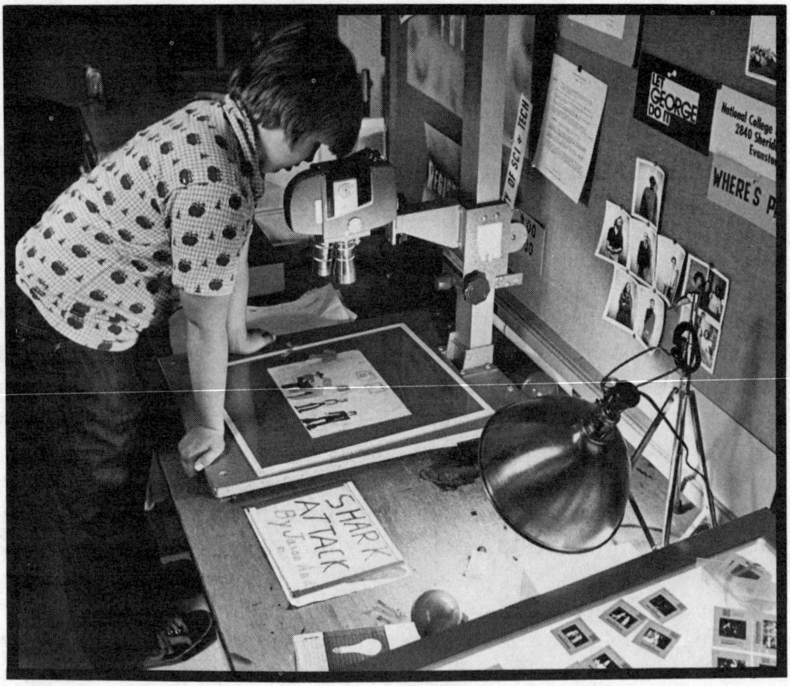
LET GEORGE DO IT
National College
WHERE'S
SHARK ATTACK

7
Movie Making

"Lights, camera, action!" is the phrase that catapults children into a process that has great fascination for most of them. To participate in the pre-production and filming of a movie not only develops composition skills and stimulates the imagination, but also helps children become more active and discriminating TV and film viewers. When you begin working with movie making, start with 8 mm. or Super 8 mm. film and a cassette recorder. Although sound movies produce a much better synchronization of film and sound, they are much more expensive to produce.

LIVE ACTION

Movie making novices will probably want to go out with a movie camera and film what they see, sequencing it at random. A much better method, though, is to compose your film in advance, deciding on the sequence of scenes and either sketching these out on story board or writing a script before shooting. Some films will call for costumes and stage props—these should be arranged for ahead of time. If actors are to be in a film, they may need some coaching prior to each scene to learn what actions and gestures are necessary. If everything is prepared, your series of shots will be better able to tell your story.

When you work with your student film makers, encourage them to describe each scene in as much detail as possible before the shooting, noting camera positions and angles, sound effects to be added later, dialogue, voice-over interpretation or whatever. Help them set up their scenes in such a way that they achieve the desired suspense, mood, nuance and focus they want. Then, when they show their film, they can either add the sound effects and voice as the audience watches or play a tape they have previously made.

ANIMATION

Super 8 mm. animated film making is really an extension of still photography. A series of still photographs are made and sequenced to give the effect of movement when the film is projected.

Recommended Equipment
- A Super 8 mm. reflex camera equipped with a cable release and preferably a zoom lens and light meter
- A sturdy tripod
- One or two floodlights properly matched to the film (indoor or outdoor)
- A series of cutouts or objects that can be changed slightly between each set of film shots, and any background material

What Movies Are

To realize that motion picture film is basically a series of still pictures, look at a strip of an old movie film and note that it is like a set of slides, only smaller. Each frame has a separate still picture on it, sequenced in the order that the movement that was filmed actually took place. At the side of the film are sprocket holes that fit on the wheels of the camera and the projector to advance it through the machines.

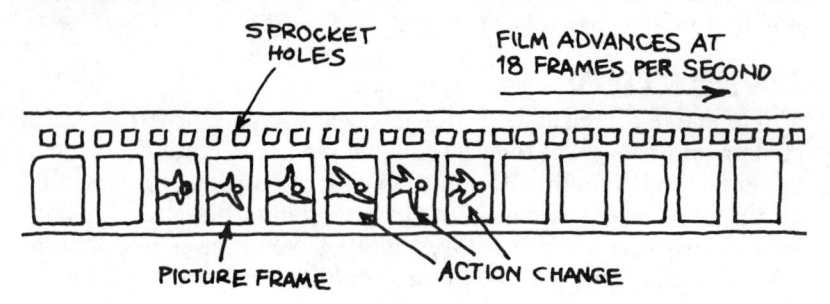

In live action film making, pushing the camera trigger down advances the frames or single shots at the rate of 18 frames per second. The film is projected back at this same rate, so the motion is shown at the same speed it was originally made. Unlike live action film making, however, the procedure for animation is to make the film at a much slower rate than it is eventually shown at. The frames or single still pictures are generally exposed one at a time or in two- to five-frame exposure spurts. After exposing one to five frames, the object being filmed is moved slightly, and another frame or set of frames is shot. So, although what is being filmed is really a series of still shots, when the shots are projected quickly one after another, the effect is one of continuous motion.

Planning the Film
As with a live action film, each shot and sequence of animated film should be planned in advance. A story board, rather than a script, generally provides the easiest way to work out the action. A story board can be as simple as a sequentially numbered series of 3" x 5" cards, each with a simple sketch of a scene on it, laid out on a table to indicate the order in which things are to happen.

When your sequence of sketches has been laid out, check it closely: Can you tell what is happening, what you want to show? Do you need to add other shots to the sequence to make it more clear? Would a different arrangement be better?

After the story board is complete, you're ready to set up the first scene. At first, flat objects or cutouts from paper are preferable. Construction paper people and animals with arms, legs and heads hinged with brass fasteners or commercially made cutouts with changes in clothing are easy to manipulate. Play-Doh or clay objects also are a good idea because their shapes can be easily altered.

Try an experimental roll of film before shooting the final work. It is usually better to take several shots of the same layout before changing the picture slightly. Although this is a little jumpier than making minute changes between each of the shots, it lessens the number of changes you need to make (at 18 frames per second one minute of animated film would need 1,080 changes in the picture).

Another way to speed up the camera work is to quickly depress the trigger for a short burst of filming rather than to use the cable release and take a series of one-frame-at-a-time shots. This will result in slightly jerky movements when the film is projected, but it is better for all but very mature or experienced students because the single-frame-at-a-time process is tedious.

Procedure for Filming
When your film is planned on a story board, the cutouts or manipulatives are ready and a first test roll of film has been shot and evaluated, you are ready for the final filming. (When you work with your students, the process is best done in groups of three—one child to operate the camera, one to animate the manipulatives and a third to keep track of where they are on the story board. It is easy to get mixed up, especially if there are interruptions.)
1. Decide on a shooting location and set up the camera and tripod, taping the legs to the floor to prevent accidental movement. Focus the camera on the location.
2. Get a larger piece of background material than you actually need, and lay it over the film location. Be sure the legs of the tripod do not show in the filming area.
3. Clamp lights to the backs of chairs or set up regular light stands, if you have them, so a maximum amount of light will illuminate the shooting area. Check the exposure meter built into the camera to be sure your light supply is adequate. If not, you may need to move your lights closer to the shooting area or add more lights.
4. Load the camera with Super 8 mm. film and check for proper exposure through the viewfinder. If shooting single frames, attach the cable release to the camera following the instructions in the manual.

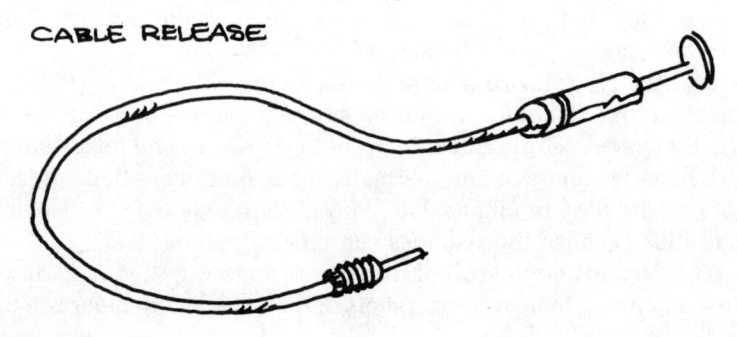

CABLE RELEASE

5. Shoot the story while another person moves the manipulatives between shots and a third follows the story board.

6. A typical roll of Super 8 mm. film runs for approximately 3 minutes and 20 seconds, so you'll probably be able to shoot several stories on one roll of film. When all the film is exposed, send it to the processing center to be developed.

Your animated film will always hold some surprises because moving from story board to film offers many opportunities for altering the original concept and hopefully improving it. As you shoot, you'll find that you may see and do things that were never imagined on paper.

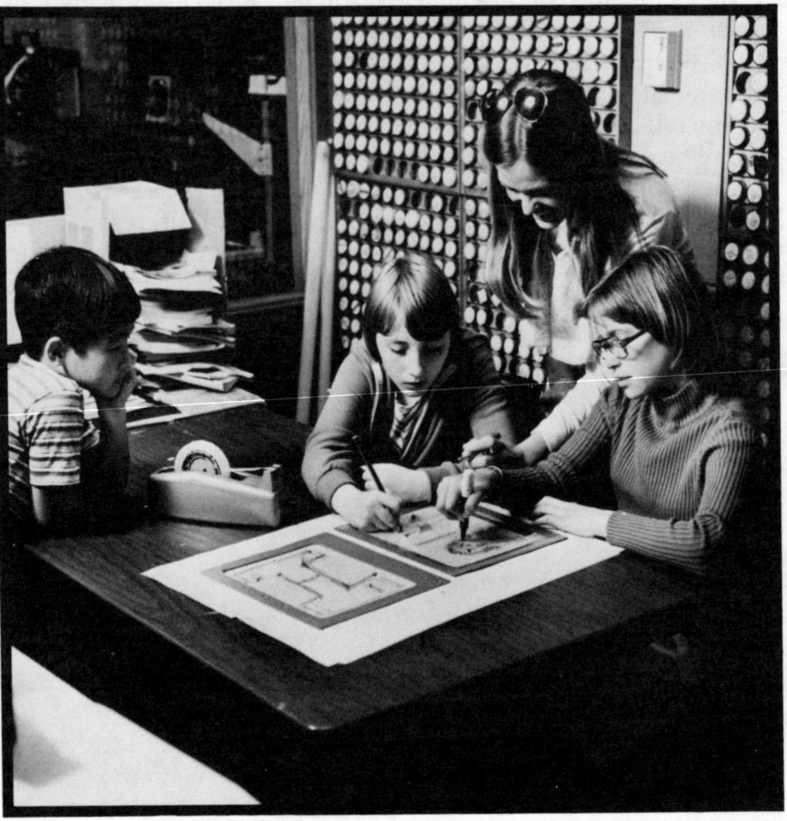

Making Transparencies

In this chapter we shall consider three ways to make transparencies for the overhead projector: drawing or tracing; the thermal process and color lifting; and making Polaroid slides. Not only is the overhead projector the most common, least expensive and easiest projector to use, but overhead transparencies are easy to make; color can be added economically and is effective; and their bright image can be projected in a fully illuminated room.

HAND-DRAWN TRANSPARENCIES

Hand-drawn transparencies cost little and can be made quickly. If you have not yet read the chapter on lettering (Chapter 4), you might want to do so before you try to letter transparencies, since the same principles apply here. Following are the materials you will need:
- The basic drawing tools listed on page 45
- Some clear acetate film
  Reclaimed x-ray film, which comes in 8" x 10" sheets, works well and is very economical[1]
- Transparency frames or mounts[2]
  You can make your own out of heavy card stock with openings cut in a variety of shapes as well as the conventional rectangular one.
- Water-soluble or permanent felt markers in various ink colors and tip widths

---
[1] A source of inexpensive transparency film is Ed-Tech Service Co., P.O. Box 407, Chatham, N.J. 07928.
[2] Your school system may have a supply for your use; if not, try a local printer.

Permanent markers tend to work better than water-base markers except in nylon-tipped Pentel pens.
- Frosted Mylar tape
Two kinds are Scotch Transparency #810, and LePages' "Invisible" #3001. Ordinary cellophane tape ages with time, becomes brittle and loses its adhesive power.

It is usually better to draw an object or idea directly onto the transparency. Occasionally, however, it is more suitable to trace an outline from an opaque picture or map or whatever onto the transparency. To trace a picture, place it face up on a flat surface, cover it with a sheet of acetate and trace it with a felt-tipped pen.

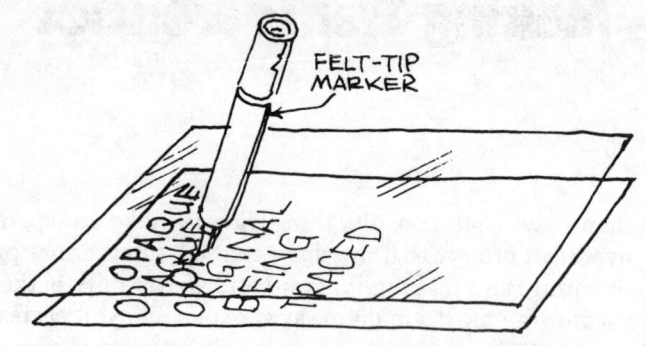

If you want a temporary transparency, use water-soluble ink, wax crayons, grease pencils or China markers—all of which can be erased easily with a soft, moist cloth. If you later decide to keep it, spray it with a clear plastic spray, such as Krylon Crystal Clear 1303. Of course, if you know from the start that you want to save a transparency, use permanent ink.

Single sheets of acetate in mounting frames are easier to use than a full roll of acetate because they provide greater flexibility. They also are much easier to save, store and find later for review. When a sheet of plastic gets scratched it can be discarded and a new one put into its frame. Temporary transparencies are less likely to get smeared if they are not rolled up. If your school has rolls of acetate mounted on the projector, see if you can get this cut and mounted into frames.

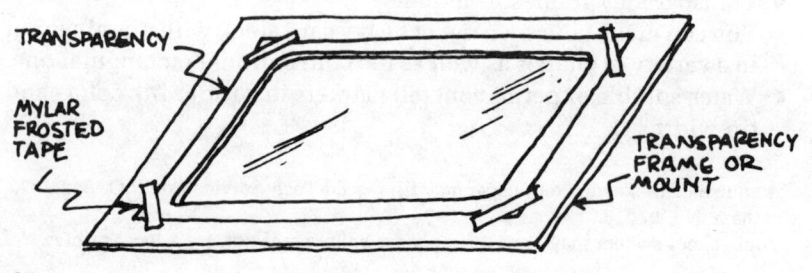

THERMAL TRANSPARENCIES

Many school systems have at least one thermal copier available either in the district office or in the local school. Whenever you want to project material that is in opaque form for group discussion and evaluation, you can use the copier to convert the material to a transparency very quickly.

Equipment and Materials
- A thermal copier
- A master made with carbon-based ink on white paper
  Usually dark or black lettering works, especially if it is done with India ink; some black felt markers do not work because their ink is not carbon-based. A #2 soft lead pencil will also work.
- Thermal transparency film (available from any 3M dealer in 8½" x 11" sheets)
  This film comes in many colors, several of which can be projected either in positive or negative form, such as the 3M black image on clear background type S88.
- A mounting frame and frosted Mylar tape

Procedure
1. Select the material to be copied—a master written on white typing paper, a commercial transparency master or a newspaper or magazine clipping. Follow the projection guide in Chapter 4 to insure that the letters will be large enough.
2. Choose the thermal film you want and place the notched part of the film in the upper right-hand corner as you look at it. Lay the film on the master; you should be able to read the printed information through it unless you have chosen a negative format film.

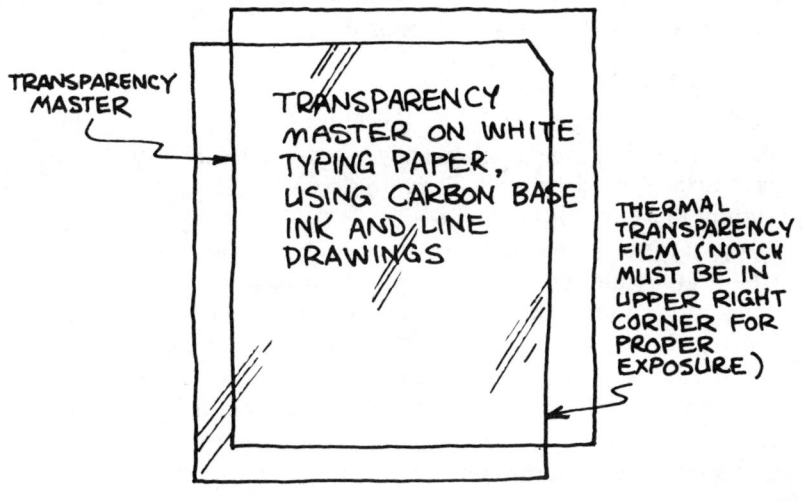

3. Set the thermal copier at the suitable setting for the type of film you are using. For best results, either follow the copier manufacturer's instruction manual or experiment with small pieces of film.
4. With the notch still in the upper right-hand corner, insert the film and master into the copier. Be sure the light comes on shortly after you have inserted the copy. The film and master are carried through the machine and return near the bottom front.

Remove and examine the film for proper exposure. If your transparency hasn't appeared, check the machine setting, film and master to be sure all are according to directions. If your master has transferred, you now have a permanent copy for projecting. To mount the transparency, run tape all around the edges and press to the frame.

TRANSPARENCIES FROM BAGGIES

Ordinary 11½" x 13¼" kitchen or refrigerator baggies or plastic garment bags used by dry cleaners can make very inexpensive or free, but serviceable, overhead transparencies. This thinner plastic is a little more difficult to handle, but the resulting transparencies are clear. You can either write on them or send them through a thermal copier just as you do other transparencies. If you do use the copier, cut the plastic to the same size as the master to be copied and insert it in the plastic carrier that came with the machine. If no carrier is available, you can easily make one by taping two heavier acetate sheets together at the top, using frosted 3M Magic Mending tape. Set the thermal copier at the normal transparency setting, usually the buff setting on the 3M copier. Insert the carrier with the plastic and the master into the copier. If you mount these flimsy transparencies in cardboard transparency frames, they are as easy to use as those made of acetate, but they are not as durable.

COLOR LIFTING

In color lifting, you actually lift the color or ink from a printed page. All you need is a sheet of clay-coated paper on which the visual you want to project is printed. Once the color is lifted, however, the original picture will be destroyed.

To test for clay-coated paper, moisten your finger and rub gently two or three times on the white area of the page you wish to lift. If a white residue appears on your finger, the paper is probably clay coated—the more clay on your finger, the heavier the coating. Well-coated papers lift best, and lighter colors project better than very dark ones. A well balanced (light and dark) picture projects best.

Materials
- The laminating equipment and materials listed in Chapter 5

- Two or three plastic or pyrex containers or trays, or at least one tray and a sink with running water
- A bottle of liquid household detergent
- Cotton balls
- Paper towels and some newsprint
- Frosted Mylar tape and mounting frames
- Clear plastic spray such as Krylon Crystal Clear 1303

Procedure

1. Select the visual you wish to lift and test to be sure it is on clay-coated paper; then rough cut it.
2. Laminate the top surface only with a hot press.[3]
3. Prepare a working area that includes either three trays or one tray and a sink.

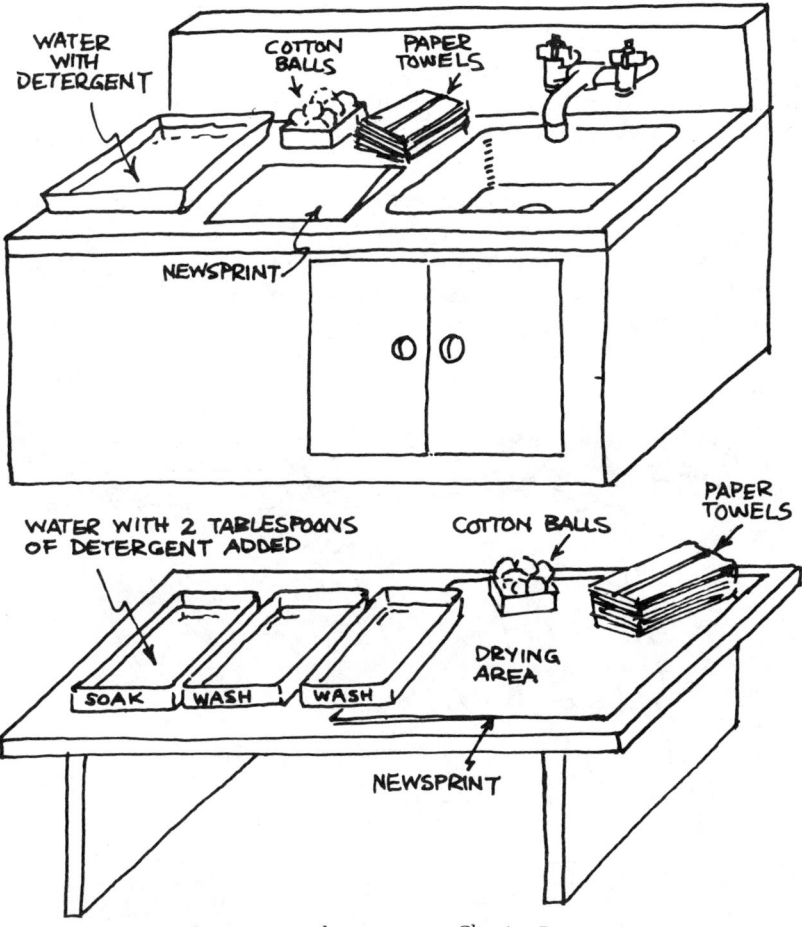

[3]For instructions on how to use a hot press, see Chapter 5.

85

4. Place the rough-cut and laminated visual into the first tray which should contain a mixture of water and 2 tablespoons of detergent. Don't be concerned that the picture usually rolls up as soon as it hits the water. Let the visual soak until the plastic lamination peels easily from the paper. Depending on the amount of clay coating this will take from one to five minutes.

5. Examine the laminated plastic you have peeled off to see that the ink has been properly lifted from the paper; if it has, begin to wash the excess clay from the back by passing it through the other tray or trays filled with water or under the faucet while rubbing gently with the cotton balls. Hold the transparency up to the light to see if all the clay has been removed.

6. Flatten the washed transparency by placing it face down on several layers of newsprint; gently rub it with a wet cotton ball until any remaining traces of clay are removed.

7. Dry the film using paper towels and newsprint.

8. Mount it in a frame that fits the picture (you may have to make one of heavy cardboard if your picture doesn't fit a commercial frame).

9. As you tape the transparency to the back of the frame along all four sides, stretch the plastic slightly so that it lies flat and taut between the frame sides. Again, check to be sure no white residue remains to make the transparency appear smudged.

10. When the transparency is thoroughly dry, spray the back surface with clear plastic spray to protect the ink and make the film more transparent.

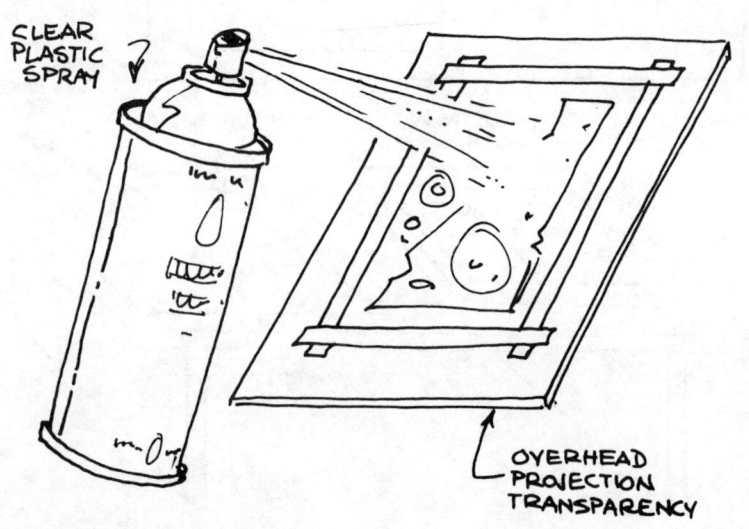

You now have a transparency of the image that was on the printed page. The process just described will work equally well in making 2" x 2" colored slides.

POLAROID 3¼" x 4" SLIDES

The 3¼" x 4" size slide is commonly called a lantern slide. If your school still has an old lantern projector sitting around collecting dust, you will be able to use it to show slides made with a Polaroid camera. Most of these old projectors have been replaced by the more common 2" x 2" slide and/or filmstrip projectors, so you may have to do some searching. While you're at it, look for some used plastic mounts as well.

To make lantern slides you will need a Polaroid camera and Polaroid negative film #46L or 146L, available in a kit that includes simple instructions and all the supplies needed to complete the process. You can buy the kit from any photographic supplier who carries Polaroid film. What you produce is a 3¼" x 4" negative that can be mounted in plastic mount #633.

The advantage of making lantern slides of this size is that a set of slides can be supplemented with drawings or with titles lettered by hand or with dry transfer letters. Young children can work with these larger pieces of film more easily than with 2" x 2" slides or filmstrips. Lantern slides are ideal for hand-drawn slide shows.

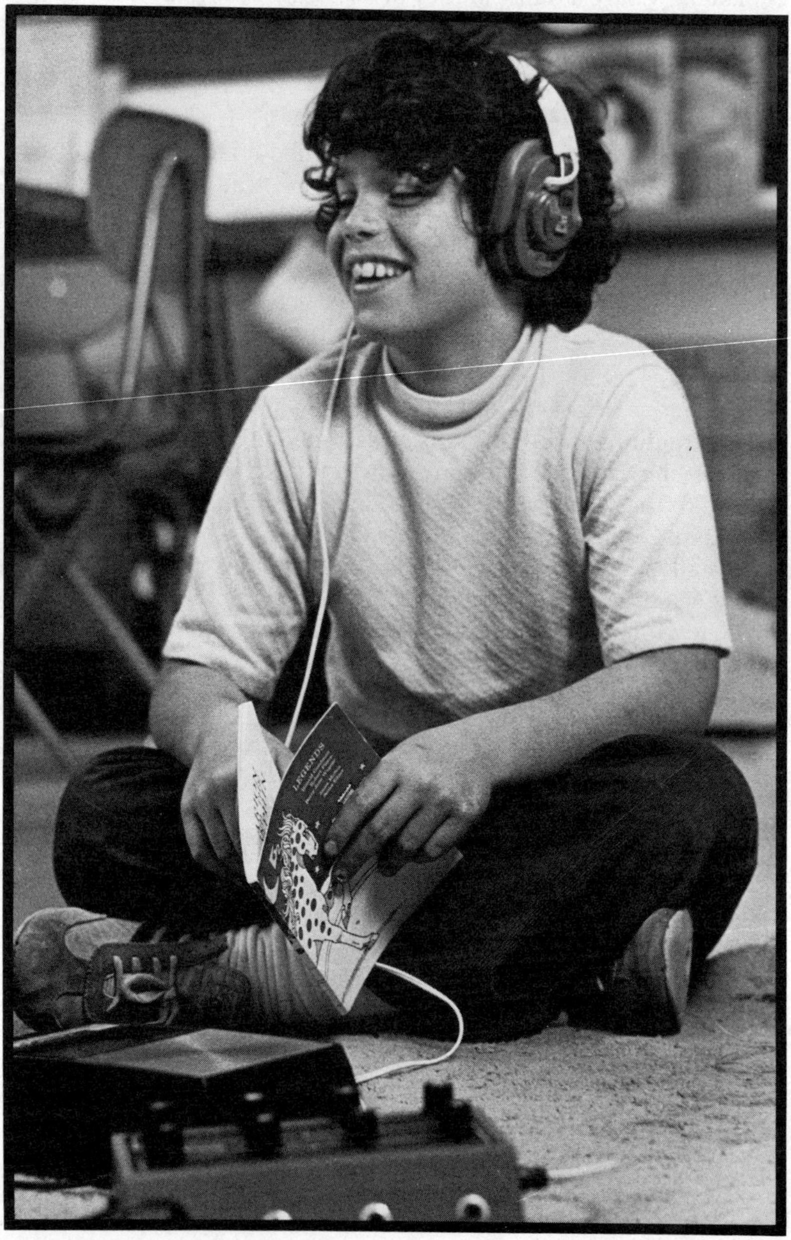

Resources

PHOTOGRAPHY
Here are a few pamphlets, books, wall charts and shows that can help you learn about photography. With experience you will become more aware of optimum exposure time, sharpness of image, effective camera angles, good and bad backgrounds, elements of composition and the need for a strong center of focus to make an impact on the viewer. All of this can be learned by exploring various forms: landscape, portraiture, still life and silhouette photography.

Books and Pamphlets[1]
The Camera Cookbook. Workshop for Learning Things, Inc., 5 Bridge Street, Watertown, Mass. 02172.

Easy Ways to Make Still and Movie Titles (AC-60)

Holland, Vicki. *How to Photograph Your World.* New York: Charles Scribner's Sons, 1974.

How to Make Good Pictures (AW-1)

Outline for Teaching a Course in Basic Photography (AT-105)

[1] All items with an order number in parenthesis are available from Eastman Kodak Company, Dept. 454, Rochester, N.Y. 14650.

Peter and His Camera (especially written for children) (AC-54)

Photography—How it Works (AT-2)

Wall Chart
Photography—How it Works (AC-41B)

Slide-Tape and Movie Programs
The following shows may be borrowed free from Audio-Visual Library Distribution, Photo Information, Dept. 841, Eastman Kodak Company, 343 State Street, Rochester, N.Y. 14650. Write to them if you want a program catalog ("Your Programs from Kodak" [AT-1]) and request forms.
Adventures in Indoor Color Slides, slide-tape (0022)

Adventures in Outdoor Color Slides, slide-tape (0023)

The Beginnings of Photographic Composition, slide-tape (008)

Photography—How It Works, movie (0345)

Snapshot Camera Handling, slide-tape (0027)

Worth How Many Words, 16 mm. movie (0238)

MOVIE MAKING
Books[2]
Anderson, Yvonne. *Make Your Own Animated Movies*. Boston: Little, Brown, 1970.

Coynik, David. *Moviemaking*. Chicago: Loyola University Press, 1974.

Cushman, George. *Movie Making in 18 Lessons*. New York: American Photographic Book Publishing, 1971.

Home Movies Made Easy (AD-54)

Horvath, Joan. *Filmmaking for Beginners*. New York: Thomas Nelson, Inc., 1974.

[2]Ibid.

Larson, Roger, and Meade, Ellen. *Young Filmmakers.* New York: Avon Books, 1971.

Lidstone, John, and McIntosh, Dan. *Children as Filmmakers.* New York: Van Nostrand Reinhold Co., 1970.

Trojanski, John, and Rockwood, Louis. *Making it Move.* Dayton, Ohio: Pflaum/Standard, 1973.

Pamphlets[3]
Better Movies in Minutes (AD-4)

Editing Your Movies (AD-26)

Making a Movie (AD-10)

Outline for Teaching a Course in Basic Movie-Making (AT-106)

Sources of Motion Picture Services and Equipment—16 mm., 8 mm. and Super 8 mm. (AD-20)

Tips on Using Kodak 8 mm. Movie Film (AD-28)

Movies[4]
Basic Movie-Making (0344 — 16 mm.) (8344 — 8 mm.)

GENERAL HOW-TO BOOKS
Bullard, John R., and Mether, Calvin E. *Audiovisual Fundamentals: Basic Equipment Operation and Simple Materials Production.* Dubuque, Iowa: William C. Brown Co., 1974.

Kemp, Jerrold E. *Planning and Producing Audiovisual Materials.* New York: Chandler Publishing Co., 1968.

Minor, Ev., and Frye, Harvey R. *Techniques for Producing Visual Instructional Media.* New York: McGraw-Hill, 1969.

Morlan, John E. *Preparation of Inexpensive Teaching Materials.* New York: Chandler Publishing Co., 1973.

[3]Ibid.
[4]Ibid.

Nicholas, Donald L., and Crow, JoAnn. *Instructional Technology: Basic Skills*. Austin, Texas: University Stores, Inc., 1974.

Oates, Stanton C. *Audiovisual Equipment, Self-Instruction Manual*. Dubuque, Iowa: William C. Brown Co., 1974.

Satterthwaite, Les. *Graphics: Skills, Media, and Materials*. Dubuque: Iowa: Kendall/Hunt Publishing Co., 1972.

Wyman, Raymond. *Mediaware, Selection, Operation and Maintenance*. Dubuque, Iowa: William C. Brown Co., 1969.